Y0-BRZ-896

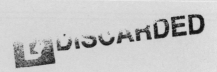

DISCARDED

THE
UNIVERSITY OF WINNIPEG
PORTAGE & BALMORAL
WINNIPEG, MAN.   R3B 2E9
— CANADA

PN
4871
.B35

The Typewriter Guerrillas:

Closeups of 20 Top Investigative Reporters

John C. Behrens

 NELSON-HALL/Chicago

Library of Congress Cataloging in Publication Data

Behrens, John C
    The typewriter guerrillas.

    Bibliography: p.
    Includes index.
    1.   Journalists—United States—Biography.
I.   Title
PN4871.B35   070′.92′2   [B]   77-3439
ISBN 0-88299-266-8 (cloth)
ISBN 0-88229-506-3 (paper)

Copyright © 1977 by John C. Behrens

All rights reserved. No part of this book may be reproduced
in any form without permission in writing from the publisher,
except by a reviewer who wishes to quote brief passages in
connection with a review written for broadcast or for inclusion
in a magazine or newspaper. For information address Nelson-Hall
Inc., 325 West Jackson Blvd., Chicago, Illinois 60606.

Manufactured in the United States of America

For my parents, Charles H. and Dorothy
M. Behrens, who provided the understanding
and opportunities to make an ambition a
reality, and to the late Don Bolles,
an investigative reporter for the
Phoenix Arizona *Republic,* who sacrificed
his life to get a story that he felt had
to be told. Don died of injuries suffered
in an explosion June 13, 1976.

Contents

"The Rolling Stone Interview: Seymour Hersh, Toughest Reporter in America," by Joe Eszterhas. Copyright © 1975 *Rolling Stone* magazine. All rights reserved. Reprinted by permission.

Precision Journalism: A Reporter's Introduction to Social Science Methods by Philip Meyer. Copyright © 1973 Philip Meyer and used here with permission of Indiana University Press.

The Associated Press Managing Editors Red Book by The Associated Press. Copyright © 1973 by The Associated Press. Excerpt from page 79 used here with permission.

Reporter's Worktext by John C. Behrens. Copyright© 1974 GRID Inc. and used here with permission.

Foreword

There was a time, twenty-five years ago, when many newspaper executives did little to encourage aggressive investigative reporting which they referred to—with a pejorative voice inflection—as "muckraking."

The perfectly honorable pursuit of old Lincoln Steffens had fallen into disrepute in the eyes of many editors who considered it an unseemly, at times unsavory, often unsafe pursuit which might cost newspapers credibility, reporters sources in government, and publishers dollars in legal fees.

Young reporters—and I was one—seemed to trust government more in those days; indeed, the American people trusted more. We had fallen into the habit of relying on government to get us through the depression, into recovery, through war, to victory.

City editors demanded that reporters "quote the sheriff"—as if citing authority gave substance to reportage. It got to be dangerous when the sheriff turned out to be a United States Senator from Wisconsin named Joseph McCarthy.

But newspaper management was more comfortable if investigative exposures were left to congressional committees or to grand juries. Newspaper executives may have been affected by the television penchant for "balance" which back then was even more pronounced than it is today. Some publishers seemed convinced that advertisers were searching for excuses to flee the printed page and turn their "message" dollars over to TV.

Of course, the prize bearing Joseph Pulitzer's name was always there as bait to lure reporters, publishers, and papers to duty. There were some rare examples of public service muckraking. Clark Mollenhoff, the Des Moines reporter whose maniacal digging had shaken the foundations of his home county courthouse, had been sent off by the Cowles organization to raise hell in Washington. And he did. Drew Pearson and Jack Anderson provided glimpses of government immorality, but many editors looked upon their syndicated column more as "dirt-digging" than valid news.

Once in a while, when a state or local official began to act like Jesse James without a pistol (as did Illinois State Auditor Orville Hodge in the mid-1950s), the local newspaper would respond (as did the Chicago *Daily News* in that case) and get the rascal sent off to jail.

Too often, however, nervous news executives—advised by corporate attorneys whose vague understanding of the First Amendment dates back to Justice Holmes' rule that nobody could cry "fire" in a crowded theater—frequently chilled reportorial initiative.

It is difficult to pinpoint when the mood in newsrooms began to shift toward more muckraking. It was helped along by "the Teamsters union story." Newspapers in a dozen communities began to report on community wrongs perpetrated by representatives of the union headed by Dave Beck and Jimmy Hoffa. Some news executives who had frowned on more investigative reporting suddenly found themselves pleased with reporters who exposed Teamsters union abuses. Nothing was more certain to get a publisher praise at his country club bar than a news and editorial attack on organized labor's hoodlum element. This time the newspaper disclosures attracted the attention of a congressional committee.

The Supreme Court's decision in *New York Times* v. *Sullivan* served to give an additional sense of assurance to newspapers. It began to be respectable and responsible, once again, to muckrake.

(Gradually good, tough reporters found themselves being encouraged by their papers to investigate and report on government corruption. Soon newspapers were moving beyond governmental stealing to other matters touching on broad public policy: the inadequacy of penal and mental institutions, consumer rip-offs, charity drive frauds, industrial contamination of the environment, abuse of constitutional rights of citizens.)

Carl Bernstein and Bob Woodward have classicized the role of the investigative reporter and Robert Redford and Dustin Hoffman have dramatized and glamorized it. Already the impact of "Woodstein"—in real life and on film—is making itself felt: journalism school enrollments have soared; newspaper personnel offices are swamped with applications; editors and publishers rarely attend a Rotary lunch without hearing from some fellow establishment member with a son or daughter in college who wants to know how to get into the newspaper business.

That sort of thing will pass. The glamour will fade as these ambitious young journalism students become ambitious young reporters and find that a president doesn't fall every administration—nor do governors or mayors, or even dog catchers.

Beyond that, many of these young people conclude, once they rub against the reality of reporting, that they lack peculiar qualities possessed by many of those who do their best work as investigative journalists.

A word needs to be said about that here, because one of the values of John Behrens' book is that it establishes, in general terms, that the modern muckraker is a special breed of journalistic cat.

I am disposed to agree with Carl Bernstein when he tells Behrens that in his work on the Watergate story he merely applied the basic principles of good reporting he had earlier developed on the Elizabeth (N.J.) *Journal.*

His approach to reporting, he says, always had been the same: "digging into things." "It's what I like to do," he says. "Most of the work I've done hasn't been Watergate-type stories, or people who have broken the law. . . . But again, I don't think you do such stories any differently." He may not. But there are many competent reporters, capable of covering important as well as routine news events, who do not have the insight, tenacity, endurance or inclination to "dig into things" as he does.

Based on observations of more than a quarter-century, I am convinced that the best of the investigative reporters either have or develop unique personal traits that commend them to this work.

I would encourage every young reporter—beat or general assignment—to approach his or her work cognizant of the "watchdog" role of the press. But some of them are not comfortable with the sort of controversy and conflict that muckraking often demands. Many of them do not have and will never develop the toughness, self-reliance, cynicism, inquisitiveness, or the simple desire to know more about the facts regarding a story than anybody else alive.

There is, within the makeup of the very good investigative reporter, the courage to stand down a bluff, the guts to confront a lie, the gall to invade unwelcome premises, the lonely inner strength to keep a secret, the sensitivity to ask the tough question, and the determination to protect a confidential source right up to and into jail.

The best of these reporters have the capacity to cajole, compromise, berate, and badger, when necessary—and at the same time to be true to their own firm, ethical understanding of what is right and fair. They have few friends who command a loyalty greater than their commitment to their work. They can be insufferable asses, unintelligible mystics, or tough adversaries when it suits their fancy or their needs.

Ben Reese, who was the veteran city editor of the St. Louis *Post-Dispatch*, once gave me his definition of the good investigative reporters. "They are always two parts bastard and one part angel," he said.

Until recently, there has been little literature to document or validate the work of these "angelic bastards." John Behrens here provides a new and personal look not only at the special sort of work that is involved in this demanding reporting, but also at some of the characters who are into it.

A. J. Liebling used to ask, "Whatever happened to the muckrakers?" Behrens provides the answer. They, once again, are with us. They are in Washington—as this book shows—where Jack Anderson, Carl Bernstein, Seymour Hersh and Clark Mollenhoff are hard at it.

Outside the nation's capital, Behrens points out, investigative reporting is presently a legitimate pursuit in Charleston, West Virginia, where Jim Haught, a reporter for the *Gazette*, brought public scrutiny to bear on the activities of elected officials. It is the same in Indianapolis where Bill Anderson worked as one of a team of investigating reporters who exposed police corruption—a labor that led to a transparently phony indictment against him. It is a legitimate pursuit in Newark—or at least it was at the time Peter Bridge was working for the late *Evening News.* He went to jail rather than reveal his source after he reported the attempted bribery of a housing official; it is a legitimate pursuit in Nashville where Larry Brinton focused community attention upon mismanagement and abuse in charity fund-raising drives. And it is elsewhere.

The newspaper business as a mirror of national sentiment has its cyclical turns. Attitudes shift and change. It can be expected that after high successes there will be press failures, abuses, and aberrations. The press is no more perfect than government, labor, management, or other institutions in society. The public appetite for more openness can be expected to dull as Judith Exner and Elizabeth Ray—with the help of the press—tell us more about government than many people care to know.

The pendulum of public attention and support can be expected to swing back against a press that becomes too abrasive, too expository, too strident, too moralistic, too investigative. Court opinions change as justices change. Publishers may again lose interest; they may lose nerve.

[If the mood turns back a quarter century and the press again takes on the bland, vapid, "observer" role of the late 1940s and early 1950s, Behrens' book will be a part of the record to establish that this was a time when public service journalism—through the intelligent and tireless work of courageous men and women—kept a busy, confused, at times apathetic public aware of its need to be an informed citizenry.]

John Seigenthaler
Publisher
The Nashville *Tennessean*

Preface

Investigative reporter. Muckraker. Scandalmonger. Typewriter guerrilla.

You have heard of the first three terms, no doubt, and you probably have your own definitions for each. The last appellation is mine. It comes from an eighteen-month investigation of the investigators which I conducted to obtain a better view of the best, close up. It comes after examining mounds of investigative stories, correspondence, notes from personal and telephone interviews, and culling the work of others. I feel comfortable with the title because I believe it applies a contemporary term to a soldier in the trenches; a contemporary figure who is emerging as the legendary hero of the second half of the twentieth century.

Webster defines a guerrilla as: "any member of a small defense force of irregular soldiers, usually volunteers, making surprise raids against supply lines, etc., behind the lines of an invading enemy army." It doesn't tax the imagination, then, to see the analogy. Investigative reporters, for the most part, are newsroom irregulars who volunteer for hazardous duty because they enjoy the excitement of going behind sensitive questions and issues of public interest and because by doing so, they believe the results will benefit society. It's a small force, certainly, considering that less than one per cent of America's newspeople are engaged in such reporting. Surprise and stealth are as much a part of the tactics and success of investigative reporting as they are on the battlefield. And what about invading armies? It is certainly no surprise that typewriter guerrillas have halted bureaucratic invasions, corporate encroachments, syndicate seizures, and a wide assortment of local and regional inequities which have injured the little guy. Like the battlefield guerrilla, the newsroom irregular destroys what he has to in order to complete the mission. But unlike the combat fighter, the typewriter guerrilla's success is positive and revitalizing, or so one hopes.

There is another significant difference, too. Typewriter guerrillas generally work alone; in small teams only when they have to. Investigative reporters, says Gene Cunningham of the award-winning Milwaukee *Sentinel*, just aren't all the same breed. The majority aren't really team players. She maintains that they don't have to be young (she's forty-six) to have the excitement, fervor and stamina to handle the work either. That Watergate was an investigation done by two under-forty reporters doesn't mean such assignments are only for youth. Nor does she believe that Watergate was in any way the end of the investigative reporting era as some have insisted. She does believe, however, that to be good and to conduct bold investigations takes a sense of realism and a dose of sensitivity that must be acquired. While toughness is the mark of top investigative reporters, she continues, most also admit to knowing the uncomfortable knot in the stomach and the sleepless nights that occur before a story appears. Even the most confident reporters are tense with the knowledge that their story carries the threat of possible jail sentences for some, the loss of jobs for others, and the obvious possibility of court action against the person who wrote it.

The aspirations of most investigative reporters are different, too. Middle-management workers in the corporate world—including a majority of reporters, incidentally—seek advancement within the organization even though it means accepting new roles and duties. A reporter, thus, can find satisfaction in becoming an editor. Not the investigative reporter. Most want nothing to do with the ladder-climbing games that spur some of their colleagues. They see themselves satisfied by the freedom to choose their assignments and come and go as they please together with a relatively comfortable salary. Otherwise they're ready to move on. "Being an editor," says Ted Driscoll of the Hartford *Courant*, "strikes me as dull."

Experienced investigative reporters, furthermore, are not encouraged by (nor do they attempt to encourage) the Watergate popularity of their craft. "I can't buy the mythology that seems current that so-called investigative reporting is some kind of new pseudo-science apart from the rest of journalism," Carl Bernstein tells graduating classes. "All good reporting, I think, is really the same." Clark Mollenhoff, who has spent more than thirty years handling investigative assignments for the Des Moines *Register and Tribune*, agrees. "The current craze, touched off by the intense interest in the realities and myths of Woodstein and Watergate, is a superficial faddist interest. It won't last, I don't believe," he scoffs.

What's the difference between the investigative reporter of today and the muckraker of the Lincoln Steffens era?

K. Scott Christianson, an Albany, N. Y. criminal justice specialist-reporter, offers one interpretation. Investigative reporting, he insists, isn't what he does. Reporters shouldn't use the tactics employed by police and district attorneys. That's wrong. Muckraking, he continues, is akin to those who seek to alter or totally change the system by working outside it. "What sets today's investigative reporting apart from earlier eras of muckraking is not its spirit, for both are unmistakably geared to achieve reform. Rather, it has only been within the last few years that the new creature has emerged. Investigative reporters, armed with new techniques, now are seeking to make an art of muckraking—one which will enable it to endure. . . . An investigative reporter is not a copout. He is willing to work within the system, however, to expose the system, to improve the system. Perhaps he can only say with some certainty 'I tried,' " Scott suggests.

Jack Anderson, who uses the two titles interchangeably but is probably best known as a muckraker, sees little difference in the terms or the work. "We must have a watchdog. We must have an independent watchdog, who is accountable to the people. We must have somebody who will keep an eye on government. Too many people in this country believe government is infallible . . . the government is fallible . . . people need to be informed," he says. The important words, of course, are government and system. They both really mean the same thing to Anderson and Christianson.

But New York *Times* investigative reporter Nick Gage sees his work as an investigator and writer in yet another way. "I think my strength is that I have a realistic sense and that I'm able to judge what is the little story and when not to waste my time. When it's not there I get out. ... I feel my job is to do my story—to lay out what it is—and I think the people who have the responsibility to take any action on it should take action. I don't feel it's my job to call them up and say 'What are you going to do about what I wrote?' "

And, says Gage, investigative reporters should not be chosen the way newspapers select other reporters and even some editors. "I think the investigative reporter has to be the most carefully chosen person any editor hires. Almost every story an investigative reporter does literally is going to hurt somebody. You've got to be very sure that you have a very strong person in the spot."

Hartford *Courant* reporter Driscoll believes management should offer the investigative task to the very best person(s) on the staff. "Try the best among those interested. If the investigative reporter does not produce, he should simply be reassigned. He should not, however, be pressured into a story. An investigative reporter in need of a story can be a dangerous fellow. ... His concern must be in telling the truth rather than getting a headline."

But it must be recognized that the best reporters may not be interested in doing such work once they discover the effort it demands. So says once-jailed investigative reporter Peter Bridge, now with the *National Star.* "This line of journalism has become the glamour stock of the profession. I suspect if it were known generally that investigative reporting, despite the rewards of success, is also the most backbreaking, tedious, frustrating, and nerve-racking work in the field, that fewer reporters would aspire to it.

"Investigative reporters must first of all be reporters, with all the usual sensibilities, curiosities, and skills that help define the term. But further, they must be at once less patient and more patient, because investigative reporting calls for a higher degree of skepticism than usual and a greater capacity to take time and careful study in targeting the truth. An investigative reporter must have brass, for once it is discovered what he is up to, he is bound to be confronted with solid opposition. Furthermore, even after having developed a substantial product, he must be willing to fight to have it published. Not everybody likes the results. Then he's got to defend it when it's attacked by those who may suffer by the exposures contained in the story or series."

Should the means justify the ends in getting the investigative story? Most of the investigative reporters I interviewed had difficulty accepting or defining "means" ("It's like getting a police chief to define what 'minimum force' is and when to apply it," one said) but the majority claim they strive to obtain material by using all available legal mechanisms. Some were less specific. The story and its impact determine the means used to get it, they said.

"We have a standard rule," says Charleston *Gazette* investigative reporter Jim Haught, "that on every story I break I must call the accused person first and include his explanation or refusal or comments. Also, we're leery of allegations from persons whose emotional stability we suspect—we get a lot of these kinds of situations, too."

"You make a judgment," Sy Hersh of the New York *Times* believes. "You use your instinct and common sense. . . . There are just certain people who say things to me that I know aren't lying . . . when I quote a source it means I believe him to be telling the truth, not just quoting him accurately. But then I don't fool around with sources either. You don't lie to people. It's as simple as that. You just don't play games. I find most people want to talk. Find the right persons and ask the right questions and a lot of times they give answers. Sure, nine out of ten say they don't know what you're talking about and hang up sometimes; sometimes they give answers."

Even more important, Huntington *Herald Dispatch* investigative reporter Tom Miller warns, "You get it

right, get it first, and get it good. The primary concern
is always the individuals who may be criminally, ethically
or morally involved in the investigation. Even if they are
outright scoundrels, you wonder about their family,
friends, etc. And that puts pressure of a different kind
on you. There is always a nagging fear that there was
some stone you didn't turn that may come back to haunt
you."

Investigative reporting, says Jack Nelson, Washington Bureau chief and an investigative writer for the Los
Angeles *Times,* will always involve risk and unpleasant-
ness. "One reason why many good reporters stay away
from such work," he believes, "is they don't like hassling
people nor do they want to be hassled. That's part of the
job I don't like either, but I'm willing to put up with it because I believe such work is important. I don't like confronting government figures with the fact that they have
lied about something or that they have done something irregular or illegal. It's an unpleasant experience. I don't
particularly like the sneers I get back from such people. I
don't like it that J. Edgar Hoover and other FBI officials
once tried to smear me as a drunk and a Jekyll-Hyde personality who was out to wreck the FBI. I didn't like it
that Hoover told those things to my superiors at the
Times. But I'm willing to put up with such things in the
interest of my job."

Readers, Carl Bernstein suggests, have the right to
expect that kind of courage and perseverance from the
newspaper and the investigative reporter today. "We
have an obligation to use the freedom we have," he explains. "We're just as irresponsible for not using it as
those who abuse it. And you have an obligation to demand that we be judicious in how we use that freedom. . . .
Our responsibility is to be fair and accurate and certainly
to not withold from comment and not restrain ourselves
from reporting on the activities of public officials merely

because they have not been accused by a grand jury of some crime. If accused, our function is not to adjudge guilt ... merely to report the truth."

And truth is what I sought in researching and writing this book. The truth about the way twenty of the nation's award-winning investigative reporters (and a few muckrakers) go about researching and reporting stories some people have gone to great lengths to prevent us from reading. In essence, this book is a collection of personality sketches about professionals whose work affects all of us. Armed with such closeups, I believe you have a better opportunity to evaluate the results of their work and assess the value of the typewriter guerrilla who writes articles that attack, charge, inflame, accuse, harass, intimidate, incriminate, and sometimes damage or destroy people, organizations, agencies, and governments on your behalf and mine.

As one might suspect, investigative reporters offer a gamut of personalities. Some see themselves as open, friendly people. "I'm certainly no loner," said Gene Cunningham of the *Sentinel*. "I'm gregarious as heck. And I can't understand how a loner, in fact, could make it as an investigative reporter. I think it takes an outgoing type of person that people are willing to talk to, feel they can trust—someone with a friendly instead of a stand-offish approach. I have a lot of friends who began as news sources and now are both. And I have a lot of friends who are on the newspaper staff, too. We socialize together, have poker playing round-robins and get together quite often, in fact. Loner? No way! I'm the friendly type—at least I think so."

Gene's lifestyle wouldn't work for Nick Gage of the New York *Times*. "Most people don't really know how lonely this work can be. You're generally not liked by your colleagues or let's say you feel you aren't. Part of it,

I suppose, are the arrangements you have and part of it is that you get more space—more attention. If somebody covering hospitals has got to do a story every day, for example, and you only do one every so often there's a difference, see. Of course, he probably wouldn't want to do the digging you do. Part of it basically is that most reporters like camaraderie—you know, to go to the bar across the street and trade stuff and talk shop. Which can lead to discussions you don't want to be in if you're an investigative reporter because of the sensitive things involved in your work. You just can't take those chances. Most investigative reporters are skeptical of everybody including other reporters, for that matter, so there's a feeling of mistrust, too. When you work on a story a couple of months you really get so involved you don't care about anybody else either."

Paranoia, I discovered, is common among investigative writers, especially when you probe the privacy of their lives. The tough exterior is vulnerable, I found. A prominent woman writer, asked to discuss her knowledge of an investigative reporter's lifestyle, scrawled a large "NO" across my letter, added an exclamation point and returned it. One reporter demanded a letter of recommendation before we could set up an interview and later, I was told, checked me out with another person in the newspaper field. Another took considerable convincing before he believed me when I said I wasn't a government agent and that I actually wanted the information for a book. The most bizarre, I suppose, was the investigative reporter whose newspaper insisted he was out of the country for the year and couldn't be reached. Finally, after my fourth letter to various editors and newspaper officials, I received a cryptic note from the reporter, asking for more information about myself and exactly how we had met, dates, places, etc. I sent the material and the references. A few days later, the reporter sent answers to my questions and a photo. The postmark was a community near the newspaper plant.

During the nearly two-year period I worked on this manuscript, I interviewed twenty-seven investigative reporters by phone, in person and by correspondence. Surprisingly, many provided considerable material by mail. "It gives me more freedom to say what I want and construct my answer in this instance," said Clark Mollenhoff, who sent me several bulky envelopes of information. Yet some did not appreciate probing questions about themselves or their work. Consequently, telephone or personal interviews were abruptly terminated in several instances. A few reporters refused to return countless phone messages and ignored letters (in one case, I sent six letters to the writer and had a colleague of his talk with him to no avail).

To test my own objectivity, I talked with nearly a dozen other journalists in Washington and around the country—some under-forty and others over it—to challenge my assumptions, interpretations and opinions. Some Washington reporters I spoke with requested anonymity because of their professional relationships. I have honored their requests. A variety of others from related fields volunteered their assistance through their writings and observations.

I'm indebted, consequently, for the contributions of David Dodrill, a former West Virginia public relations man now with Columbia Gulf Transmission Company, Texas; George Rasanen, Washington Bureau, Cleveland *Plain Dealer;* the late Jack Bell of Gannett Newspapers and formerly of the Associated Press, Washington; Al Nerino of the Reading *Eagle;* Michael Sheridan of the Hartford *Courant;* Malcolm F. Mallette, director, the American Press Institute, who has probably attended more seminars on investigative reporting than many investigative reporters; Bob Eddy, former editor and publisher of the Hartford *Courant*, now a visiting professor at the Syracuse University; the late Theodore Link, former investigative reporter for the St. Louis *Post-Dispatch;* and Michael Levett and Dan Noyes of the Urban Policy Research Institute of California.

And I owe sincere gratitude to twenty investigative reporters who took time to talk with me about their lives and work and to Robert Brown, publisher and editor of *Editor & Publisher*, whose periodical was invaluable in researching current events in journalism.

Finally, my thanks to Utica College reference librarians Pat Dugan, Gisele Skinner, and Sylvia Rathbun and typist Rose Palczynski. Without their help, I'd still be working weekends to finish this manuscript.

Photo of Jack Anderson taken at interview and lecture
at Colgate University, Hamilton, N.Y. March 4, 1975.
Photographer Richard Broussard.

1

Jack Anderson: A Muckraker's Muckraker

By merely mentioning one name, you can enliven the next party you attend. But use caution if you are in the company of military brass and government officials. This name guarantees animated conversation among a cross-section of your neighborhood or community; it can bring out the "tiger" in liberals or conservatives, intellectuals or blue collar, employed or unemployed. The only requirement, really, is that you live within one of the more than nine hundred newspaper circulation regions that carry his column each week.

The name? Jack Anderson, of course.

It brings out the worst in those he has attacked; it represents everything American to those who rely on him for news, views, gossip, and fact. And some do. He's the Billy Graham of media journalists, others say. Yet a number of reporters don't claim him as a fraternity brother. Some news executives, especially those in the Eastern

Establishment, scorn and sneer at his methods and revelations. His popularity among publishers who buy his United Features column is hard to assess. While they intuitively feel reader demand for his Washington Merry-Go-Round column, they're ambivalent about his work. "The column can be difficult because of the possibility of libel and remember, many small town newspaper publishers don't have libel lawyers or insurance," said a former managing editor of a community daily in the Midwest.

The fears of client papers and the controversy that surrounds each column produced in his busy, five-room suite on Sixteenth Street in Washington have been well understood by Anderson since September 1, 1969, the day Drew Pearson died unexpectedly at his farm. A corporation doing hundreds of thousands of dollars worth of business would have had all kinds of agreements on paper to protect survivors and perpetuate the name and image of the founder and the firm. Pearson, unfortunately, didn't even provide for his staff. He had kept Jack (one author believes Anderson won a power struggle with several Pearson staffers by refusing to press for a raise) with a promise that one day the column would be his. *Parade* magazine had offered Anderson a better salary and his own byline. The Sunday magazine supplement permitted Pearson and Anderson to work out an agreement so they could continue the column and their work on the publication. That was in 1954. Fifteen years later, Drew's wife accepted Jack's explanation of the promise and settled with her late husband's assistant for $1,000 a month. The same day, Anderson and an executive of the feature syndicate agreed to a five-year contract for less than Pearson had received. While the two parties acknowledged that Washington Merry-Go-Round was a household word, both realized that editors and publishers could use Pearson's death as an obvious excuse to drop it, especially since it was now being handled by a lesser known aide.

But such obstacles don't bother Jack Anderson, ex-merchant seaman and freelance journalist from Long Beach, California. His Mormon training and his super-positive attitude diminish difficulties, associates believe. Success, one could conclude, is as natural to Jack as the Puritan work ethic was to Horatio Alger. And, incidentally, they've got a lot in common. To Jack, evangelism is the real task.

"Surprising how many people across the country believe the press take things out of context," he told a crowded auditorium at Colgate University one bitter cold March night not long ago. It was one of a dozen or so lectures and public appearances he makes in a month. "That the press does misrepresent the facts and because this is one of the backlashes of Watergate we need to take a better look at the role of the press in a free society.... Our founding fathers knew about tyranny. They'd lived under it. They knew that government by its nature tends to oppress those that have power over it and they were determined, therefore, to have a watchdog. They looked around and selected the press. I'm not altogether sure it wasn't a good one. I think we had our moments of glory—we've had our moments of shame. I think we've been vigilant at times. I think we've been asleep more often. I think that, I suppose, we've had our martyrs ... but we've also had our prostitutes."

His message has the drama and fervor of a fundamentalist circuit rider. He puts his five-foot ten-inch, well-proportioned frame and resonant voice into each paragraph (two years in the South as a Mormon missionary gave him the opportunity to listen to and watch some of America's best revivalist preachers). He punctuates with dramatic pauses and inflection and booms his message when he makes a point ("In those days, when you competed with a passing freight you learned how to yell"). His gestures are as patented as his talk; he removes his glasses with the care of an Ivy League college professor, and he brandishes file folders with the flair of a used car salesman. He's part investigator, part dramatist, and part actor—and certainly he's the granddaddy of the sophisticated muckrakers in America today.

"The government has never been suppressed," he insists. "During the worst of Watergate, Richard Nixon got his story out. He was able to talk about anything he wished for as long as he wished on all three networks during prime time without commercial interruptions. His press conferences were carried verbatim in our leading newspapers. His statements got front page. The American people knew Richard Nixon's version of Watergate. But in this country, the press has other obligations, too. Our functions are to dig out the secrets of government and give them back to the people who own the government....I've seen dictators rise in my twenty-five years at the ringside. I've never seen a dictator rise anywhere but what his first move was to muzzle the press; a dictator must control the flow of information to the people. I say to you that on the day that the government controls what I write, on that day, we lose freedom of the press, and on that day, my friends, you have lost your freedom."

The words, the nasal sound which trails off those vowels, and the cleverly executed wry grin and glower are pure Andersonian. But they sell on the circuit what the column sells in cliché-sprinkled meat and potatoes in print. It perhaps rankles reporters who don't have Anderson's national exposure, lecture contracts, sources, and income. It infuriates those who have conscientiously attempted to track down an Anderson exposé.

"Jack enjoys that muckraker reputation, but I do

not regard him as America's No. 1 investigative reporter. Neither does my boss nor some other reporters I know," says a Washington reporter for a major daily. "Anderson in my view is often shallow and leaves me with questions. He does serve a purpose though. Some of his stuff comes in from irate sources who feed him. It runs sometimes before it has been checked thoroughly. We had an experience with Anderson in which he wrote a piece about political pressure applied to an FBI agent to stop an investigation. After we had thoroughly checked, the Anderson piece proved to be filled with distortions and too much reliance on FBI sources. I would never write a follow up on an Anderson piece with the same degree of confidence as I would, say, with Woodstein, Nelson, or Polk."

He's been rebuked by professional organizations and he's apologized in the now-famous Senator Thomas Eagleton incident (during the 1972 presidential campaign, Anderson broadcast an erroneous story that Eagleton, the Democratic vice presidential nominee, had been arrested for drunken and reckless driving during the 1960s).

Recently, the National News Council upheld a claim by the Accuracy in Media (AIM) group that an Anderson column in August, 1974, concerning attitudes of students at the International Police Academy about torture contained misrepresentations and out-of-context material from student papers. Council staff members on a visit to Washington to investigate said that Anderson's quotes "do in fact misrepresent the attitude of the students toward torture as set forth in their papers [and] in addition . . . that all five papers were written in the years 1965–67, a fact not mentioned in the Anderson column" (which had given the impression that they were reasonably contemporary). Again, Anderson denied the charges although he did admit that the column in question could have been better handled.

And Jack has also denied stories of financial arrangements with those who could benefit from a positive story or his silence. Such allegations were made in 1973 by former White House Counsel John Dean. According to Dean, Anderson and Drew Pearson had been paid $100,000 in 1958 to write favorable articles about Cuban dictator Fulgencio Batista. Dean said the information was contained in a memo written by special White House counselor Charles W. Colson. "I have never accepted money to write favorable columns about Batista, Castro, or anyone else," Jack replied. "My columns are a matter of record. I wrote no favorable columns about Batista in 1958 nor Castro in 1961."

Yet newspaper colleagues are more inclined to criticize than sympathize. Copley News Service columnist Neil Morgan believes that such incidents have caused a shift in public opinion. "People are fed up with the attitude represented by Jack Anderson's ballet dance in the Eagleton affair—that it is more important to lynch a suspected scoundrel in the media than to check the facts first and be absolutely fair and accurate. And that attitude is all too widespread."

While he denies such implications, the Washington columnist does admit he occasionally errs. "It doesn't mean that we are always right. We've all made mistakes. I tell my reporters that I want the facts just as they are, not as they hope they are, not even as someone may tell them they are, I want the facts as they are. Well, that's a lot easier to say. It's a lot easier to order than it is to accomplish. But we try."

His candor, Anderson staffers and ex-employes say, is what most people do not see. To those who deal with him daily he's an open man who doesn't spare himself six days a week but does, like a practicing Mormon, spend his Sundays with his family—wife Livvy, and nine sons and daughters—in church. "All humans make mistakes," former Anderson aide George Clifford said in an *Argosy* magazine article in May, 1974, "and Anderson takes this into account when deciding whether to skewer an errant public servant. On the rare occasions when a mistake does creep into his column, Jack never tries to pass the buck to an assistant. He takes the blame."

He talks easily to audiences about his approach to journalism and issues and the network of sources he uses—a list some investigative reporters believe to be one of the most extensive in Washington. At Colgate, for instance, he was relaxed, affable and even struck a Bill Buckley stance at times. Dressed in a conservative gray pin stripe, he shook hands with ten or twelve newspersons and visitors gathered in the dusty chapel basement and sank into an easy chair to answer questions. He was an assortment of personality traits: cajoling, paternal, caustic, sympathetic, dogmatic and retiring. You walked away with the sensation that you'd met a human laser beam; his blue eyes literally pierce each person he meets.

"Investigative journalism is always trying to uncover what's being covered up," he says in answer to a question. His voice is barely audible at times. "I don't trust what I get from people, whether they are in government or out. We simply can't afford to take the word of the most trusted sources at times. When a trusted source tells me something, I don't necessarily accept it. I want it documented. We've got to be able to back it up. Or it's just part of the story . . . not enough to actually get a true picture. If you publish that part of it, it's not that you don't try to get the whole element; perhaps the government is trying to obscure that. You must try to nail it down. However, I do think it's safe to break the ice even though you don't have the whole story. After all, we may not yet have the whole story on Watergate. You can't wait around until you get the final item. News is like a serious story with a chapter each day. What you missed today hopefully you'll get tomorrow. We will frequently write a story about an event after talking to a dozen people who know about it. Then we will print it. When it appears in cold print, ten other guys' tongues will suddenly loosen and the whole story comes into perspective. They will say to you things they wouldn't tell you before the story broke."

Sources, he adds, are an individual matter. His twenty-nine years in Washington and his national status have opened more doors than many rivals realize, a newspaper executive says. "Actually I try to develop my own sources and after getting them I construct my own stories. I think you let the story take you where it leads and you dig out all you can," he explains.

What investigation has satisfied him the most?

He doesn't pause to remember. "Usually it's the last one I worked on or the one I'm working on now. . . . We're always working on something and that's the one that usually absorbs our attention. Generally, those that have accomplished something. I always feel better about the ones where something is done as a result of my story. The FBI-CIA disclosures are an example. I began writing about this five years ago and it created a response. There's no mistake about that. The FBI and CIA issued statements, denials, for the most part. Even though there were press conferences—former FBI Director Pat Gray held one—and we were stirring up the FBI, CIA, and the Secret Service, I was frustrated because we weren't accomplishing anything. We weren't stopping their practices (preparing dossiers of prominent citizens without evidence of an illegal act).

"Now, suddenly we've got Congress investigating and we've got the CIA and the FBI going up to Capitol Hill. . . . I think that it was the post-Watergate mood that brought it about. They're going up now and admitting what they were denying three, four, or five years ago when I first wrote the story. Going up and confessing that 'yes, J. Edgar Hoover did keep dossiers.' Specifically, it was four years ago that J. Edgar Hoover had in his office secret dossiers of prominent people. That was vigorously denied. Now we've got the present director of the FBI saying that he recognizes the problem and wants to change it."

The leakiest agency or department in Washington, Jack continues, is probably Congress, with the White House close behind. "Congress, if you want to take a body of people, would probably lead the list because of the numbers of people. The White House, though, is forever giving stories to their favorite correspondents in order to further their politics. Here again, we're not sure of the quality of those leaks. Sometimes, you're suspicious because of the location of the leak. For example, we were given a story about the armed forces—it was leaked to us—and we began investigation and found out that the guy who leaked it to us was misrepresenting. We wound up publishing a story that resulted in an investigation of the guy who leaked the story and we never did divulge his identity because it was a confidential relationship. We just found out enough information that made him look bad and he wound up the subject of the investigation. They still don't know that he was the one who originally leaked it to us; in fact, he would be the last one at this point that they would suspect because he turned out to be the victim of his own story. Why? Because he thought he could sell us his point of view and we weren't going to check it out . . . and we did check it out."

But "selling" and "buying," a subject of much concern to such major media as CBS, the *National Enquirer,* the *National Star,* and others, aren't a part of Anderson's arrangements. "I've never paid for information and I don't disclose sources," he says, closing the subject with silence.

His day usually starts about 7:30 A.M. when he drives to the studio to tape a daily show. Then he goes to the office where he may spend two to three hours before lunch on the telephone. While he's more likely to have a sandwich and Coke at his desk, Jack sometimes eats out, choosing the Empress Restaurant on Connecticut Avenue or the posh Madison Hotel, where he has become the resident celebrity. When he returns to the office it's to take phone calls or make them, sometimes until 7:30 P.M. He usually goes home for dinner with Livvy and members of the family not yet in college. To some, Jack's home is more like a residential Holiday Inn. The doorbell and telephone give it a cacophonous sound along with the continual movement of family and guests. Somehow though, after he finishes dinner, he can go to the study and work until past midnight, oblivious to the rush of activities and crush of people in the house. The grass may not be cut, the garden hose may still be where it was last spring, but it doesn't bother homeowner Anderson. Some evenings, though, are spent in any number of Washington landmarks or more secluded places, meeting sources who have stories to tell or evidence to give him.

It's Livvy who gives her famous husband the chance to concentrate on his work. The daughter of a West Virginia mining family whom Jack met while she worked at FBI headquarters, she manages their massive eight-bedroom frame and fieldstone house in Bethesda, Maryland, writes the paychecks, pays the bills, handles the bookkeeping for Anderson, Inc., and sleeps until noon to meet the rigors of each day.

While the majority of investigative reporters in Washington make less than $40,000 a year, the stories about Anderson's income are as legion as his income sources. One reporter who has been familiar with the Washington press corps believes that the ambitious columnist-investigator grosses $200,000 to $300,000 a year. And, like his predecessor, the reporter adds, he pays some aides less than top-ranked reporters on major papers. But Jack's income potential in any year hinges on a myriad of ventures. On the lecture circuit where he spends a number of days each month, his fee is estimated at $2,000 to $2,500. His successful journalistic coups— the publication of secret White House documents about the Nixon Administration and the Indian-Pakistani war and the famous Dita Beard-ITT memo—caused Random House publishers to give him a $100,000 advance for his book, *The Anderson Papers*. Add to that a company formed in the early 1970s to package national radio and television programs and his outside interests (Anderson and CBS reporter Connie Chung were among a group that filed to open a new District of Columbia bank, the Diplomat National, for the Asian-American community; he has an interest in the weekly Annapolis (Maryland) *Capital*, a fraction of a Daytona Beach, Florida, motel, and a mid-town Washington office building) and, consequently, his yearly earnings could be a conservative estimate.

Anderson has disposed of his $2,000 in stock and resigned from the board of directors of the Diplomat Bank to avoid a conflict of interest. The columnist acted quickly in late 1976 when the Miami *Herald* disclosed that a portion of his column about South Korean religious leader Sun Myung Moon was dropped because of a federal investigation examining a Moon aide and a South Korean businessman's 40 per cent control of the new bank.

Tax assessors in several states are also aware of the affluence of Jack Anderson. In addition to his $100,000 Bethesda home, he has a fifty-acre farm in Washington County, Maryland, a half-interest in a tract of land near Fredericksburg, Virginia, and a luxurious summer place in Rehoboth Beach, Delaware.

While he shuns the aristocracy and attacks those who pay little or no taxes, Jack sometimes sounds more like landed gentry than a middle-class citizen.

"I'm opposed to welfare," he told the Ivy League audience in Yankee-flavored upstate New York. "You see, I was brought up in the West where my Mormon parents taught me to stand on my own two feet. They taught us to work for whatever we got. They taught us that you got stronger legs climbing mountains than coasting down them. But they taught us to also help our neighbor. But we were taught that the best way to help him was to give him a hand—not a hand out. So fundamentally, I'm opposed to welfare. But, my friends, if the government is going to give subsidies, if the government is going to give welfare, I would rather give it to the poor."

And what does he think of journalism after Watergate?

"It's more holier than thou . . . I think so. The cream of the crop of our reporters are at the White House, supposedly. Not one of them had anything to do with Watergate. Not one of them had anything really to do with reporting the biggest story in White House history. I don't think that's anything the press ought to be proud of. I suggest what's wrong is that these reporters adopted the views of the people they're writing about. They've become a part of the Establishment they cover."

Photo of William Anderson by William A. Oates,
Indianapolis *Star* photographer.

2

Investigative Reporting Is Bill Anderson's Apex

When Governor Otis Bowen was told of the indictments of two Indianapolis *Star* reporters on charges of conspiracy to commit a felony, he was, aides said, "surprised and shocked."

No wonder. The governor, along with other *Star* readers, had been following the chronicle of corruption about the capital city's police force for days and he was probably stunned to discover that the investigators had been arrested by the investigatees!

To *Star* reporter Bill Anderson, a forty-nine-year-old World War II combat veteran (Okinawa) and one of the two newsmen indicted, the court order came as no real surprise. Anderson, Coordinator Richard Cady, and Harley Bierce—the *Star*'s investigative team in 1974—were up to their eyeballs in investigating corruption in the Indianapolis Police Department. They knew the stakes were high; they always are when reporters take on law enforcement people.

The muck was so bad in Indianapolis, however, even police informants repeatedly asked reporters if they were really prepared to finish the investigation; if they were prepared to take the consequences. Some of the information, the cops said, was unbelievable considering Indianapolis' reputation as one of America's cleanest cities. But principals in the cases were ruthless enough to try anything.

It didn't take long to discover that the police informers were right. The series, which began February 24, 1974, with a long story headlined "City Police Corruption Exposed/ Millions in Graft Bribery Fixes/ Six Month Probe by the *Star* Shows Crime Is Protected" reverberated in Indianapolis and neighboring cities. The fallout from the stories affected many at all levels of the department.

"Certainly it was the most rewarding story I've worked on. We developed it, had to fight for our journalistic life, were threatened, arrested, and then proven right in our stories. The results, while many, have not gotten to the core of the problem yet but we think it may come later. All top police were replaced as was the director of public safety," Anderson says with some satisfaction. He adds, "It was our story from the very start—no handouts, press releases, just good hard news that we dug out. And, of course, there was real satisfaction in bringing about needed change." A sense of irony, too. Anderson was a winner of the Fraternal Order of Police award ("I helped a police cause in 1957 which I suppose a few would like to forget. But they never asked for it back.")

Bill's knowledge of the city and its people and his experience as a reporter proved invaluable as the story progressed. A lifelong resident and a graduate of Indianapolis schools, he joined the *Star* in 1950 when "investigative reporting" was a term rarely heard in the newsroom. It was more often called "interpretive reporting" and was frowned upon by many editors. He left the newspaper field in 1956 to give radio a try as news director of a local station. Twelve years later he returned to the *Star* after giving up broadcasting, a job as press secretary to the mayor of Indianapolis, and even serving a year as advertising director of a city bank. Investigative reporting was "in" and Anderson began handling such assignments within weeks after he rejoined the paper's reportorial ranks. His stories on the police department and crime brought recognition within months. He won local and sate awards from 1969 to 1973.

The police corruption story, he knew, was much bigger and deeper than any he had probed before.

From the beginning, reporters and Managing Editor Robert Early had little to substantiate what they heard. Policemen not involved in the scandal didn't want to provide information until they had a guarantee there would be an honest, thorough investigation. The cops knew that the newspaper couldn't assure such results even though *Star* management wanted the same thing. No one knew how far the corruption had spread. They feared what actually developed later: a publicized probe which swept out the majority yet left remnants.

It was Anderson, a police beat man ("I love my work. Always have. My father was a printer at the *Star*, my two brothers are in journalism—one is a columnist in Long Beach, California, the other is an assistant publisher with the Worrell Group in Florence, Alabama.") who passed the first word of trouble to City Editor Lawrence Conner in early 1973. The *Star*, a conservative paper that rarely crusaded, was the morning half of the Pulliam's Indianapolis newspapers in a city well known for its low crime rate. In two weeks, Anderson and Cady had produced enough evidence to demonstrate that three hundred of the city's eleven hundred police force were involved in "willful and systematic" corruption.

Anderson, Bierce, and Cady, dubbed the "A-B-C

team" by colleagues, spent more than a year gathering material and cultivating sources. Their information filled two full-sized filing cabinets. It contained tapes of five to thirty minute length, interview notes, and signed documents that the recordings, usually made in the presence of two reporters, were accurate. The *Star* investigators interviewed more than four hundred persons, including sixty policemen and sheriff's deputies and a number of former police officers. Said Gerald Healey in the December 21, 1974, issue of *Editor & Publisher* magazine, the reporters' information-gathering efforts were persuasive. "In questioning the forty-eight informative police men, the *Star* team looked for corroboration of their stories of the strongest type."

The inquiry consumed more time than any member of the team had ever spent on a single story. "During the investigation we worked from 10:00 A.M. until 2:00 A.M. the next morning at least six days a week," Anderson says, always adding a rejoinder. "I've been married twenty-five years and I have a very understanding wife. She knows I have late hours at times and she knows the risks that are involved on stories like the police investigation. I spend as much free time with my family as I can."

The *Star* management kept federal law enforcement fully informed during the course of the investigation. Editors presented their reporters' findings to then Assistant Attorney General Henry E. Petersen, head of the Criminal Division of the Department of Justice in late November 1973. Though preoccupied with Watergate, Petersen alerted the Federal Bureau of Investigation and, a month or so later, the Bureau entered the Indianapolis case. The Federal Strike Force in Chicago had already begun assembling its own information. The details, said a *Star* editor, "read like the old-time dime novel."

Thirty days later, the *Star* published the first of two

hundred fifty articles in a seven-week period concerning their findings. The major headline stories speak for themselves:

"30 Policemen Tied to Brothels; Took Protection Money, Referred Women to Jobs";

"Report Bootlegger Payoffs on Sunday Sales";

"Connections Aided Vice Parlors";

"Police Linked to Drug Traffic";

"Police Involved with Pawnbroker Convicted as Stolen Goods Fence";

"Police Case-Fixing Racket Told."

The stories were devastating to the elected and the electorate. The *Star* told its readers that vice operations in Indianapolis during a ten-year period totaled $40 million annually, with illegal narcotics trade well above that figure. Detectives took money to fix court cases or free suspects, including two arrested on charges of murder. Links were established between political figures and vice cops protecting massage parlors which may have involved up to a dozen officers. An illegal fencing operation handled stolen goods, and there was evidence seven policemen participated in thefts while on duty.

And that wasn't all. There were shakedowns at three Indianapolis taverns; detectives setting up burglaries and taking money from those arrested on burglary charges; there were abuses in departmental collections for the needy and thefts from the Police Athletic League funds. Perhaps more frightening, however, was the unexplained disappearance of confiscated weapons from the police property room.

The stories did produce results though. The articles, together with the Department of Justice's assistance, triggered formal investigations and swift changes within Mayor Richard G. Lugar's police force. The chief of police, a deputy, and the city safety director were the first to go. The chief of the department's vice and narcotics squads were transferred and dismissals removed rank-and-file officers found guilty of specific crimes.

The changes, while satisfying to the A-B-C team, had brought months of tension and apprehension. There were threats, for instance. "Anderson, Bierce, and Cady could get themselves killed if they continue this," callers warned, letting the reporters conjure the way a policeman or those sympathetic to the department might get rid of them. The reporters knew they were followed by plain-clothes and uniformed cops and their conversations were tape-recorded at times by persons they couldn't identify. The legal machinery as well as law enforcement officials might try to sidestep a continuation of the probe, their sources warned them.

Again, their sources were correct. After a new Indianapolis police chief was appointed he hinted that the *Star* investigation should end following the prosecution of the officers charged with corruption. The chief's statement stiffened the resistance to the A-B-C team's efforts to pursue the probe. The reporters detected another attempt to whitewash the case and leave other questions unresolved. But the newspaper refused to accept the chief's suggestion. Furthermore, Anderson said, the continuing investigation now revealed that four police officers appointed to inquire into other charges "had shady records." Even more incriminating was the newspaper's discovery of files that indicated the Indianapolis Police Department had been under surveillance by other law enforcement officials for more than a decade.

The first grand jury failed to get into the more serious questions and, after brushing aside fourteen issues related to corruption, it was dissolved. The second set of jurors, however, introduced more confusion than clarity by indicting Anderson and Cady on charges of attempting to bribe a policeman, presumably in exchange for information. The charge, said the *Star* managing editor, Robert Early, was absurd. "I get just a little nervous when I see a reporter challenged in attempting to get the news. I believe a reporter has standards he must observe but he still has to get out and have his freedom so he can get the news as it is," he noted when the pair were released on their own recognizance. The indictment was introduced to the grand jury by the same prosecutor the reporters and their newspaper had criticized for laxity in dealing with corruption. And he was up for re-election.

But the indictments were later dropped because of a legal technicality; the grand jury had been improperly empaneled, according to a newly elected prosecutor. It had excluded persons over sixty-five, the district attorney said, adding "I believe this indictment fails for lack of evidence. . . . I believe they (the grand jury) were either mistaken or misled." The *Star* insisted it was nothing more than a frame-up shortly after the charges had been handed down. In a front page editorial, the newspaper told its readers that the jury's action was "a clumsy effort to undermine the credibility of the investigating team and of a series of articles about police corruption and its coverup by the prosecutor's office."

The consequences, Anderson insists, were well worth the personal and professional risks. There were accolades and rewards along with their own self-satisfaction. The team has won more than a half-dozen national awards, among them the coveted Pulitzer for 1975, Sigma Delta Chi, National Headliners honors, and the $5,000 Drew Pearson prize for excellence in investigative reporting.

But more important battles are still ahead, Anderson tells audiences these days. The father of six wants no part of a rocker and reminiscences, although he admits some of his old sources on the police beat might be more suspicious and consequently make his efforts more difficult. "The free press is really under attack," he told a group of editors not long ago, "and you have to fight back, really keep the heat on the politicians. . . . It will take another year or two to discover how the corrupt Marion County (Indianapolis) system works and there will be efforts to silence the *Star*. There already have been. Some policemen regard me as a traitor, others admire me, some still speak to me, a lot of them don't."

Bill Anderson knows, though, it's what you learn to expect when you take on the title and responsibilities of investigative reporting. "I'm different from others I suppose. I have been a reporter for twenty-five years—I want nothing else. I don't feel qualified to be an editor and to be placed at a desk would be horrible for me. I enjoyed days as a police reporter more than others I ever had in this business. I'm a rare person—I'm happy doing exactly what I want to do in life."

He also accepts the special status of "investigative reporter" in the newsroom where little is sacred and a great deal is scoffed at. "It's hardly a peer group," he says. "Sure, we are secretive by necessity really but we enjoy an excellent relationship with other staff members. In fact, we're far from loners. We enjoy the company of others so we can talk about something other than what we're doing daily."

A reporter needs outside activities and diversions to handle the concentration, patience, and recall demanded for an average day with an investigative team. But what's a day like when he's not working on a specific investigation? The routine is like this:

"I was awake at 7:45 A.M.—remember, this is a morning paper. My hours are in the afternoon really. Anyhow, I have two cups of coffee while reading the *Star* along with a smoke or two. I'm a grouchy person for the first hour or so, just ask anyone around me. I don't eat in the morning when my wife and children are there. I take a third cup of coffee to the bath with me as I shower and get ready to go to work. It helps me collect my thoughts and get ready for the day.

"I got in early this day for a Criminal Court hearing which took two hours. Called my associates, met for lunch with them and discussed our current project. There are four of us presently on the investigative team headed by Cady. We are all working on the same project—wiretapping. I returned to the office at 1:15 P.M. and answered three telephone messages. Only one-half of the calls are really worthwhile. I kept a 2:00 P.M. appointment along with Bierce to discuss our project with an informant. Cady is writing tomorrow's story.

"When we return from our appointment we have a short informal meeting with our city editor, Lawrence Connor, to inform him of our progress. We normally work a week ahead except when we're in on breaking news situations. After that, it is an hour or so at the county recorder's office checking ownerships. Back to the office at 5:00 P.M. I find several more telephone calls to be returned and I make several of my own. Two of them were to set up more meetings. We then read today's story before it goes into the basket. Two persons I couldn't reach I called later after I got home. Had dinner with my wife and three youngest after 7:00 P.M. and then made my calls. Had a drink with my wife, read until 12:30 A.M., and then went to bed."

Regardless of the hours, the occasional danger and the pressure, Bill doesn't see his job as something out of the ordinary. "There's nothing special about it. . . . It certainly is something that is needed in journalism and I'm happy I had something to offer in this area. The *Star* has always been investigative, I believe, but the team concept here is somewhat new. It's good to be a part of it. Reporting is all I want to do. Investigative reporting is the apex."

Photo of Carl Bernstein courtesy of Carl Bernstein.

3

Carl Bernstein: Investigative Reporting Is Simply a Label

Carl Bernstein is an Aquarian.

But you don't need a horoscope or his birthdate (February 14, 1944) to sense it. He's noticeably gregarious, obviously self-confident, interested in new ideas, persuasive, and a natural psychologist who makes use of his knowledge of human nature.

Such traits were powerful pluses in uncovering Watergate, one of America's most sordid political scandals. And it was such characteristics—not a horoscope—that caused Harry Rosenfeld, assistant managing editor for metro news at the Washington *Post,* to select Bernstein and team him with Bob Woodward to cover the second-rate burglary that resulted in one of the major stories of the century.

"We made careful, meticulous assignments, calling first for personnel records and selecting those with skills to track down, while keeping mature perspective. We especially looked for persons who were error-proof. We laid it all out for them. . . . We anticipated violent denials and assaults on our paper. In short, from beginning to end, we knew where we were at. We prepared ourselves for every contingency," Rosenfeld told an Associated Press Managing Editors meeting.

Because it was a burglary, *Post* Managing Editor Howard Simons had first called Rosenfeld, the editor in charge of local news. "We were the ones set up to handle such news. . . . At our shop, District of Columbia Editor Barry Sussman had called Bob Woodward. He had very little experience but he had shown an uncanny ability to root out stories that other people couldn't. . . . Bernstein, that Saturday (June 17, 1972) was working on the Virginia staff where he was to remain a week or ten days, and he was volunteered by his editor, Tom Wilkinson, to work up profile material on people arrested at the Watergate."

The rest, of course, is journalism history. Bernstein and Woodward won virtually every journalistic award, including the Pulitzer Prize, and received one of the highest fees paid to a pair of working reporters to write a book about their coverage of President Richard Nixon's White House (Their book, *All the President's Men,* earned one million dollars in paperback rights and will pay them each $45,000 a year for the next five years after settlements with the publishing firm, Simon and Schuster, and their literary agent).

But "Woodstein," as Woodward and Bernstein were called in the *Post* newsroom, were still a somewhat risky combination, Rosenfeld says. "From a working editor's point of view, I have found over the years that to get your people to work well, your good people to work well at least, you have to create a universe for each one. In this universe, they can do their best work. Woodward, from the first day that we hired him, showed his ambition, heart, and productive work, and so too did Carl Bernstein. For a long time, though, finding a suitable universe for Carl had been difficult."

To those familiar with the *Post* newsroom, Carl's search for a universe during the pre-Watergate days involved a number of colleagues and editors. Ambitious, opportunistic, and arrogant were milder terms used by associates to describe his behavior. He gained a quick reputation as a chronic borrower of money and cigarettes and one whose lifestyle was in constant motion. He had a penchant for posh living—gourmet restaurants and buying sprees for sound systems and record collections—which friends found he couldn't resist. He ignored the advice of those close to him about money management until success introduced the need for a financial adviser after the book was published.

His work hours were irregular. He would appear the moment a major story broke in the newsroom, usually armed with sources and background. He was a virtual almanac of the city and its people and he rarely waited to be asked about it. He also made it clear to most editors he didn't like routine stories or assignments. He liked to develop his own articles and he turned off those who tried to supervise, assign, or edit his copy.

Carl's search, in fact, had been erratic before he joined the Washington *Post*. Academic work, he admits, was disappointing. He smiles as he tells commencement audiences that it took a hastily convened conference of teachers to nudge him through a District of Columbia high school. His frustration with the educational system ended in 1964, however, when he dropped out of the University of Maryland to go to work. He had sandwiched classes with work as a copyboy at the Washington *Star* for three years. An offer to become a full-time, full-fledged reporter on the paper caused him to drop plans to get a degree. Months later, he left the *Star* and joined the

Elizabeth, N.J., *Journal*, an independent daily with a circulation of 63,000.

A former *Post* colleague who had become editor of the *Journal* enticed Carl to Elizabeth, where he was given freedom to write the stories he wanted. But a year later, Carl was eager to return to Washington. In 1966, the *Post* gave him the chance. However, the tradition-bound *Post* did not offer him the freedom he had enjoyed at the *Journal*. Consequently, those first two years back in Washington were precarious for Carl, his associates and supervisors, one editor recalls. Friends hoped that events in 1968 might change things. The restless newsman served a year in the army and married another *Post* reporter. But the turbulence of the times was reflected in Carl's lifestyle. His marriage ended in divorce and professionally he struggled with the frustration that frequently besets a young reporter on a great newspaper dominated by superstars.

He had already proven his worth in the competitive business of reporting; a story he wrote for the *Journal* had won the 1966 New Jersey Press Association's first prize for general reporting. Not a bad beginning for a college dropout. But instead of new opportunities—chances for advancement—and stories of national consequence, Carl became the *Post*'s roving reporter specializing in Virginia politics. It was a job that offered good experience but virtual obscurity if you consider the impact of Virginia politics on the nation. "The last time Virginia was of national interest was when Thomas Jefferson was in office," a wire service correspondent said with a shrug. June 17, 1972, transformed Carl Bernstein's world.

Yet, while Watergate turned it around for the prematurely gray reporter, he doesn't believe he's changed. "I don't see myself any differently than my first days," he says with a noticeable Southern inflection. "The team investigative reporter was always there. I've done some

pieces which conventionally are called investigative. I'm
talking about what reporting is: the, best obtainable
version of the truth. Well, when you try to find the truth,
you're investigative. It's a game of semantics, I suppose . . . I don't think such labels are important."

And he's understandably proud of his own accomplishments—stories he wrote sans-Woodward in the pre-
Watergate days. "I tend to feel good about a lot of the
work I've done on the *Post*. One of the first things I did
in fact with another reporter was a series on slum property in the District of Columbia in 1966–67. . . . I did a
long, long profile of a company town in southwestern
Virginia. I did a piece on a group of people called tri-
racialites—that's part-black, white, and part-Indian—
and how they evolved their own society. Peculiar to their
experience, I remember, was the fact that they had been
discriminated against by minorities—black and Indian,
for example, as well as whites. All kinds of things were
discovered in doing that story but really the approach
was the same."

Bernstein's approach has been the same since his days
on the Elizabeth *Journal*. In fact, he can't remember
when he didn't use the techniques more popularly known
today as investigative journalism. "I've always ap-
proached especially long pieces by digging into things.
It's what I like to do. Most of the work I've done hasn't
been about Watergate-type stories or people who have
broken the law or anything of that kind. But its been
about how people live . . . but again I don't think you do
such stories any differently. Sy Hersh [New York *Times*
investigative reporter] and I have talked about this. I
think we disagree to an extent. The one thing that so-
called investigative stuff really is, is actual painstaking
work. It's hard work in the sense that people like Sy,
Woodward, and myself, and I'm sure others, spend a lot
of time with records and going through ten thousand

pieces of paper and whatever to find a certain little thing. Such work requires patience certainly if you want to do a definitive piece whether it be on the Washington Redskins or Watergate."

Reporting, Carl insists, is frequently getting along with people. People you like and don't like. "It has a lot to do with dealing with people. . . . The whole thing is a human pursuit. It involves how you are able to get them to trust you and whether you are able to extract through careful listening new information from what isn't. I don't think that reporting has too much to do with life-styles; it has to do with how good your reporting is. I don't think the fact that somebody has long hair or rides a bike has anything to do with it except that I think you obviously want people to feel at ease with you. If you're going somewhere in cutoffs and a fatigue jacket you could tend to make someone feel ill at ease . . . on the other hand, someone else could feel perfectly at ease with such dress. It could create empathy for you."

Contrary to popular reports, Bernstein doesn't think that he and Woodward were chosen to cover Watergate because one was a better writer and the other a better researcher and interviewer. "I tend to think that both of us are pretty good reporters. I do one kind of writing better than he does and he does one kind of writing better than I do. He's quicker and can block something out to show where it's going and I'm probably slower and a little better at saying what we mean. My writing might be more polished at times. . . . We talked out subjects and, at the same time, we both got to the typewriters. Woodward's style is to get something down on paper and then talk about it. I guess maybe I'm that way, too. It's not a science, you know, it's something you do. I like what we do and the way we've worked."

The Watergate story, he adds, had few instances where news leaks were used. "It just didn't involve the technique of leaks per se. It was much more than that and much more legwork. It was looking for the little piece of a larger mosaic and fitting it in."

What was the most difficult period in getting the story? "I think July 1972, when the whole thing looked like some kind of Caribbean adventure. It took time to really sort out and find perspective then."

Their success in handling the Watergate assignments was influenced, he continues, by their total independence from Washington officialdom. In the traditional sense, they were simply skeptics turned loose to ask questions. "The Nixon Administration was able to call press credibility in so much question for some good reasons, I think," Carl tells audiences today. "If you go back to the beginning of the Nixon Administration in 1969 you might remember that then Vice President Agnew gave a speech in Des Moines, Iowa, in which he said it was time for the media to turn their critical facilities on themselves. And perhaps, not for the same reasons as Mr. Agnew, I rather subscribe to that idea today. I think that perhaps the best advice of all to those of us in the media was given by John Mitchell, also at the beginning of the Nixon Administration, when he told the press to 'watch what we do and not what we say.' And perhaps because Woodward and myself were metropolitan reporters and not members of the more prestigious national staff at the *Post,* because we were unaccustomed to having sources in high places who we ate with in fancy restaurants, perhaps because we hadn't become so close to sources that we became unthinkingly almost a part of the Administration—perhaps it was because we'd never had those experiences that watching what people were doing rather than what they were saying came naturally.

"Too much Washington journalism and particularly too much of the journalism practiced on perhaps hundreds of small newspapers in this country has traditionally been a skill more akin to stenography rather than reporting."

While Managing Editor Simons feels both reporters were given basic freedom to handle the Watergate stories in their own way, precautions had to be taken, too. "Remember, we were dealing with sources who had to remain anonymous; with two young reporters; and with material that, if wrong, could massively damage not just the Washington *Post* but our profession. Accordingly, from the beginning . . . the editors adopted three rules to govern the publication of a Watergate story in our newspaper. The first is that any set of significant facts must have come from at least two independent sources. As a result of this rule we never carried some information. . . . The second rule is that one or more of the top editors of the newspaper must read and approve the story before publication. And the third rule is that a story on Watergate from another publication must be independently verified by our reporters before we give the story prominence."

Did such controls bother Bernstein?

"As much as I have a lot of disagreements with editors and sometimes look at editors as a necessary evil, they're always needed. I can't imagine doing anything without the editors. If an editor's good, he helps the story. If he's bad, he hurts it. We always need good editors. We need them for writing because you're too close to the story sometimes. They're needed for perspective, too. And I say that as somebody who historically has had huge fights with editors: news editors and book editors. I think the role of the reporter is much too confining. I think reporters should have much more to do with conceptualization of coverage which is traditionally that which editors—not reporters—worry about. I think reporters ought to have more to do with that. I certainly see editors, though, having a real function."

But even with disagreements and pressure from within the newsroom, the most intolerable situation, Bernstein declares, was the external forces. When stakes are high, ethics and principles are sometimes forgotten words. Did Watergate conspirators and governmental agencies try to squash the efforts of the *Post* reporters?

"Sure they did . . . in a number of ways," he retorts. "The most effective thing they did was attempt to destroy our credibility and that was undertaken out front. We were told by our best sources that we were under surveillance. We never saw any physical evidence of it, though. Whether we were or not . . . all we know is what we were told."

Their persistence despite the obstacles impressed normally cynical competitors on other major newspapers. "What more can be said about these guys?" said a young bureau reporter for a Midwest daily. "In my view, the key to their success was that they were opposites and they were more tenacious: Woodward mature and to the right; Bernstein liberal and more radical. They balanced each other perfectly, along with the great help of *Post* editors. I can find no fault with such a combination or the Watergate investigation."

But there were errors.

"I can think of some times we were wrong about some things," Carl volunteers. "Some were not of the highest standards in retrospect. I can think of a story where we were just plain wrong. It identified some people associated with the story and it was wrong. And we still haven't found out about that one either. I won't forget it."

Neither will Rosenfeld. "On the Haldeman story, we said that the grand jury had heard testimony from Hugh Sloan, CREEP treasurer, that Haldeman controlled the fund along with four others. We were wrong. There had been a misunderstanding. That is to say, we were confident that the substance was true. Haldeman controlled the fund. We argued among ourselves. Do we pull back? How far do we pull back? Woodstein did a foolish thing then. They cornered some of their sources in semipublic circumstances and there was a great deal of retreating. Some of us urged that we stand by the story and Bradlee [Ben Bradlee, *Post* executive editor] decided to do just that. We urged Woodstein to find still other sources and nail it down or discover new evidence that we were indeed wrong. Very soon they turned up more confirmation and we were able to print still another knowledgeable person's assessment that it was a Haldeman operation."

Did they hold articles back while reporting the Watergate investigation? "There are always times when you're not sure of a story and you're obligated to hold it . . . yes, we held stories. It happens all the time, every day," Carl replies.

However, the reporters didn't withhold ideas.

"Anything we knew about during the investigation, we wrote. Seems to me that's the way you do reporting," Bernstein explained. "You know something, you put it on paper . . . you don't walk about with it in your head. And as for anything else that might be just speculation, based upon one little piece of information somebody brought you that might be true or might not, I think it's really destructive to talk about that. . . . We found a fair amount of information during the early period when there was a lot of material which was leaked to us and other papers, indicating that this was some kind of right-wing conspiracy, to the extent that the New York *Times* and the Washington *Star* wrote it as hard copy. *Times* implied it more than writing it straight out. But we were able to establish rather quickly that it just was not the case."

It is the uncertain first days of Watergate that disturb Carl in retrospect. "The media (since Watergate) are in the midst of an orgy of self-congratulation largely about Watergate. I think it's very important some of the mythology be dispelled. And that it be made very clear that the orgy is not justified. There are more than two thousand reporters in Washington and until after the first Watergate trial—the trial of the underlings and the hired hands—there were only fourteen assigned to cover Watergate on anything like a full-time basis. And I must say of those fourteen, most were engaged in following the day-to-day events that happened in court rooms, statements by the White House staff, filing papers with lawyers, and so on. In other words, looking at the surface events related to Watergate, Woodward and I took an opposite approach. The *Post* took an opposite approach. But I think there's been a mythology that's developed that I would like to dispel because what we did at the Washington *Post* was not that extraordinary. Particularly in terms of how we reported the story.

"In fact, Woodward and I used the most basic, empirical techniques similar to those we first learned when we were very young. We knocked on doors, we talked to people at the bottom, which is to say secretaries and file clerks rather than starting at the top . . . and there was nothing glamorous about it. But what was really extraordinary about it . . . was not the methodology but what was yielded by the methodology. And I guess we all recognize now the implications of that information for the country and our profession were immense."

But Carl doesn't advocate the trend to popularize the role of the investigative reporting in media.

"I don't buy the mythology that seems current, that so-called investigative reporting is some kind of new pseudo-science apart from the rest of journalism. All good reporting, I think, is really the same. It's an attempt at attaining the best version of the truth. You have to realize that merely recording official pronouncements in stenographic style and reproducing them accurately without subjecting them to any test for the truth is not reporting. That's the case whether the official pronouncement is made by Ron Ziegler, Gerald Ford, Henry Kissinger, the mayor of the city, or the president of a university. In reading a newspaper you should demand that we who put that newspaper out should go beyond that stenographic function and that we do what reporting is about."

The over-thirty reporter who, along with Woodward, took a leave of absence from the *Post* after Watergate to write their second book, claims such political subterfuge is a lesson for the media and every citizen. "It's simply this: we have an obligation to use the freedom we have. We're just as irresponsible for not using it as those who abuse it. And you have an obligation to demand that we be judicious in how we use that freedom. During rather dark months when we were being attacked by the White House, a new mythology held that somehow the responsibility of the press is to be judicial rather than judicious and that we have to show the same kind of restraint that the courts do.... That somehow we should be bound by federal rules of criminal procedures rather than by merely the highest standards of our profession. And nothing is further from the truth. Our responsibility is to be fair and accurate and certainly not to withhold from comment and not restrain ourselves from reporting on the activities of public officials merely because they have not been accused by a grand jury of some crime. If accused, our function is not to adjudge guilt ... merely to report the truth ... the facts."

And what of the future for the Pulitzer Prize winner?

Not clear. "I'm going to work, that's the answer," he tells audiences. "I feel good and I don't have much to complain about. Sure, there have been offers. I'm a reporter, though."

But others feel the future of Woodstein is even more

vague than his answer. Said a newsman in Washington who has followed their work: "Woodward and Bernstein are no doubt millionaires now, when you take into consideration money earned from their book and movie rights ... I think their real problem now is fighting boredom and trying to come up with an encore."

The popularity and overnight success of their Watergate work for the *Post* made them instant national— perhaps international—personalities, but observers believe they've handled their fame quite well. Only one flap has surfaced involving the pair: did Woodward actually steal Bernstein's girl? According to *Editor & Publisher* columnist Carla Marie Rupp, the woman in the triangle was Frances Barnard, Washington correspondent of the Fort Worth *Star Telegram,* and the story was avoided in Woodstein's book *All the President's Men.* Woodward married Miss Barnard in November 1974. After the ceremony, the new Mrs. Woodward tried to set the record straight. While she had met the two reporters at the same time along with others at a restaurant across from the *Post,* she merely bicycled with Carl several times, she said. Carl married *Esquire* writer Nora Ephron in 1976.

Said a newspaper source who followed the careers of Woodstein and their respective mates: "Their credentials could make a team that could equal Jack Anderson's muckrakers."

Photo of Peter Bridge courtesy of the Utica College News Bureau.

THE
UNIVERSITY OF WINNIPEG
PORTAGE & BALMORAL
WINNIPEG, MAN.   R3B 2E9
CANADA

4

Twenty Days in Jail Hasn't Changed Peter Bridge

Peter and Anne Bridge look at the photograph and break into nervous smiles and affectionate glances. The picture shows a very pregnant Anne Dubyna Bridge—an attractive housewife raised in upstate New York—and her two children being interviewed by a horde of newspeople. There's worry written all over their faces.

The photo gives you the impression she doesn't want to think about the questions she's being asked but she realizes she must. Few women could have withstood the ordeal as well. Her husband was out of work. His newspaper, the Newark *Evening News,* had closed several months earlier. Worse, he was in jail. He had refused to answer questions put to him by an Essex County, N. J., Grand Jury investigating corruption within the Newark Housing Authority—corruption he had written about in an investigative story. The jurors and County Judge H. Curtis Meanor, a one-time sportswriter for a New

Jersey paper, were especially interested in one sentence in his story: "Mrs. Pearl Beatty, a commissioner of the Newark Housing Authority, said yesterday an unknown man offered to pay her $10,000 to influence her vote for the appointment of an executive director of the Authority."

What irritated Peter was the lack of investigative work done by the prosecution. "They didn't send out a single investigator in this so-called investigation. Not a single one. They interviewed forty-one witnesses, but they never investigated a single thing. Nobody talked to me before this subpoena was issued. They just dropped it on me," he told the Associated Press Managing Editors meeting later. The prosecutor demanded that Peter surrender notebooks, deliver contact lists, expose sources, and violate "my personal and professional ethics." And while events were being shaped week after week in that New Jersey county courtroom, the young investigative reporter found himself fighting a cause few others considered important.

"This whole thing started on May 19, 1972 . . . when I was subpoenaed. Actually from the first, media ignored it," he explains. "They just didn't believe I would go to jail. In fact, after I was in jail . . . a friend came to see me and said, 'I don't believe it, I just don't believe it happened' . . . and I remember saying, 'Ed, I'm here . . . you're here' . . . once the jail doors close, it becomes a news story because it's actually happened. Suddenly it hits the A-wire, there are pictures and there are interviews on TV with my wife and kids. . . . Oh God, you know it fell upon my wife because I wasn't around. . . . I was out of circulation behind bars. Before I went in, I told my wife that this would probably happen and she said, 'What will I do?' and I said, 'Tell the truth . . . just tell the truth' . . . and that's what she did and she carried it off pretty well. The truth is she bore much of the burden of this. She was answering phone calls way after midnight. . . . You see, newsmen have no politeness about them. If the spirit hits them after midnight, they'll call you. That's the nature of the news business. How do you handle this? You keep telling the truth."

The court fight began innocently enough. The irony, of course, was that the litigation occurred in a state where the law offers newspersons immunity from such prosecution. However, New Jersey courts ruled that the state statute protecting confidentiality only covered the source's identity. And since Peter had already identified Mrs. Beatty, according to the prosecution, the court had legal authority to investigate other matters pertaining to the case. Similar cases, in fact, were being tried in states with and without shield laws. "A dozen newsmen around the country are . . . facing possible imprisonment (at least in theory) including the three main figures in the historic Supreme Court case: New York *Times* reporter Earl Caldwell, former Louisville *Courier-Journal* reporter Paul Branzberg, and Massachusetts TV newsman Paul Pappas. Among other reporters in legal trouble, Los Angeles newsman William Farr is confronting an indefinite jail term for contempt because he refused to identify his source for a story concerning the trial of Charles Manson," *Newsweek* told its readers in its October 16, 1972, issue.

But Peter had no intention of answering Judge Meanor's questions. He had answered many (about thirty-five of eighty-eight), but he adamantly refused to divulge whether Mrs. Beatty had offered a description of the person who tried to bribe her, where the bribe took place, or if there were threats other than those reported in the article. His refusal to answer the queries, the judge said, did not free him from responsibility under the circumstances. He was in contempt. Yet, the judge also told him the "key to the jailhouse was in my pocket," Peter remembers. "He said had I attributed that quote to an anonymous source that I would have been home free. I would never have been called before the jury. But because I named that public official which, in my mind, was the responsible thing to do after all, I was jailed." Said the jury: "By the reason of the position taken by Mr. Bridge, our investigation was hindered and is incomplete . . . It is the opinion of this jury that when a journalist is in possession of facts which will aid in the pursuit of truth, he stands in no favored position . . ."

Consequently, Peter Bridge, the unemployed newsman who still believed in the principle of confidentiality and journalism ethics even if he lacked the means to back that belief (the defunct *Evening News* parent company Media General provided preliminary legal expenses but dropped the case ten days after Peter was jailed), spent twenty days in the Essex County Jail. He had the dubious distinction of being the first reporter jailed following the U.S. Supreme Court's landmark decision in June 1973, which said that newsmen may not withhold confidential information from courts of law. He was jailed twenty-four hours after the high court voted eight to one to reject his appeal, in fact. He was released unconditionally on October 24 by the New Jersey Supreme Court after the grand jury was dismissed.

"When I went to jail there was so much furor about it that they bowed their bloody heads and decided to get me out of there," he insists. "It was just too much trouble. . . . But what I'm concerned with is not so much press freedom as with the free flow of information. A reporter is bound—if he's serious about what he's doing—to go beyond the released information. . . . I find reporters concerned about that throughout the country; editors and publishers are not really concerned . . . reporters are. I guess the only way we can awaken people to it is to risk going to jail. If by intimidation or jailing or whatever, these agencies are successful in getting reporters to stop reporting the way they have and publishers are too frightened to allow such reporting, then sources will dry up and the public will get only press releases. We simply won't get enough information. Press releases do not contain the complete story. Presidential administrations have sought to control the news for decades this way. Lyndon Johnson, John F. Kennedy, Eisenhower, as well as Nixon tried to control the press."

Reporters, he insists, must be adversaries to public officials "not always in an unfriendly way, but they must play an adversary role. As soon as they stop playing such a role, they become public relations people for all kinds of public agencies. There is a considerable amount of that kind of thing in the press today. There's too damn much of it."

That was the advice Peter gave students one day when he visited his alma mater, Utica College, in upstate New York. He had been raised a short distance away in Waterville. A small farm community that doesn't remember Peter Bridge as easily as it recalls George Eastman of Kodak fame, Waterville was once called the "Garden City of New York State." He attended a Catholic school in Utica—St. Francis deSales—for a year and then transferred back to Waterville to complete his education. He entered the Army in the mid-1950s and acquired a background as a Korean language expert in military intelligence after attending the army's Monterey Language School in California for forty weeks. He graduated sixteenth in his class. At Utica College, however, his record was not so impressive, say faculty who remember his college days. His adviser, Professor Raymond Simon, thinks Peter surprised a lot of people with his notoriety. "Peter took several journalism and public relations courses with me in the four years he was at UC in the late 1950s. I recall him to be somewhat of a 'loner' with a strong sense of independence and self-confidence.

He was not particularly outstanding, but he was one who questioned unwarranted assumptions and glittering assertions. I can't say I expected he would go to jail for a principle but I strongly respect his ultimate defense for protection of a newsman's sources of information."

Utica College, at the time, did not have a journalism program, Peter remembers, and he graduated with a degree in public relations. "With such a degree it was hard to convince some editors of your journalistic ability but I had some purely journalism courses at UC, too." His first job, however, was in public relations on the staff of the Utica YMCA. After he received his degree, he went to work as a reporter on the Endicott, N. Y., *Bulletin,* which folded seven months after he started. Days after the *Bulletin* closed its doors, he went to work for the Oneonta *Star,* a morning daily in southeastern New York. A few years later, he joined the Newark *News* as an investigative reporter.

Peter moved into investigative work eagerly and with an awareness of its impact. During his college years he had watched the city of Utica torn by scandal and corruption. A state investigation, called by the governor, brought resignations and criminal charges against a number of Utica officials. And it was the Utica *Daily Press* and *Observer-Dispatch* that uncovered illegal activities. A team of reporters and editors won a Pulitzer Prize for their efforts.

Newark offered similar challenges, Peter found, and he dug into city hall troubles as well as the city's underworld. He worked with a colleague on a book entitled *Mafia Talks* which bared the inner workings of the Cosa Nostra in New Jersey. He felt satisfaction, he says, when his investigative work helped bring charges against Newark Mayor Hugh J. Addonizio, who was sentenced to ten years in jail and fined $25,000 after being convicted on sixty-four counts of conspiracy and extortion.

Investigative reporting—the painstaking search for the missing pieces—is what it's all about, he believes.

"This line of journalism has become the glamour stock of the profession. I suspect if it were known generally that investigative reporting, despite the rewards of success, is also the most backbreaking, tedious, frustrating, and nerve-racking work in the field, that fewer reporters would aspire to it.

"Investigative reporting must first of all be reporters, with all the usual sensibilities, curiosities, and skills that help define the term. But further, they must be at once less patient and more patient, because investigative reporting calls for a higher degree of skepticism than usual and a greater capacity to take time and careful study in targeting the truth. An investigative reporter must have brass, for once it is discovered what he is up to, he is bound to be confronted with solid opposition. Furthermore, even after having developed a substantial product, he must be willing to fight to have it published. Not everybody likes the results. Then he's got to defend it when it's attacked by those who may suffer by the exposures contained in the story or series."

But obtaining the facts and digging out evidence of criminal acts are not the most exciting part of this work. "I've often said that if I had a dollar for every voucher I have handled in search of just one, I would be a millionaire, and if I got overtime for every hour I have sat and pored over dull records, I would never have to work again. But an investigative reporter develops a thick skin and waits for the inevitable without letting up on his effort. For every Watergate, though, there are millions of research efforts that go absolutely nowhere."

Part of the success of those who handle investigative work, Peter says, lies in understanding the value of the personal interview. "The crucial tool is the simple, direct question. Very often you will hear an interviewer on TV or radio preface a question with a long statement or some kind of preamble, so that by the time the subject of the query comes up, everyone (including the reporter) is confused. I prefer the simple form such as 'Did you kill your wife?' Notice I did not ask 'Did you or did you not kill your wife?' "

Interviewees react in a myriad of ways, and instinct has to determine how a reporter responds to answers. "You've got to listen carefully and have a good background to know what's good material and what's useless. I rely on my own intuition and senses because experience has shown me they are more often reliable than my logic. Not so incidentally, I have found my intuition to be a powerful tool in my line of work, allowing me to go places where others might not; ask questions others might not have thought about; and to manufacture a product unlike that of any of my competitors. For example, in late 1969, the U.S. Attorney's office launched an investigation into the affairs of the city of Newark. I had been covering that city for a year and knew most of the people likely to become part of the investigation. I labored hard and long to uncover facts that no other reporter on the scene, including some from my own paper, were able to. The investigation, I might add, was being covered daily by more news organizations than I knew existed: The New York *Times*, New York *Daily News*, New York *Post*, the three television networks, two wire services, every radio and television station in the greater New York area, a number of national publications, and assorted foreign news organizations, to name a few. On every single day the story was running, I was able to write stories that had never occurred to any of the other reporters. They had people (the *Times*, for example, had an eighteen-member team) and I had a sense for the story. It finally reached the point that I was greeted each morning by a contingent of newsmen usually with the question, 'Well, are you going to tell us about today or do we have to wait until tomorrow's *News* comes out?' AP eventually reached an agreement with my paper to obtain page proofs before the paper hit the street for a few minutes beat on my stories. They agreed to attribute the stories to the *News*. In the end, my editor told me he had not seen such good reporting in a decade. I got a sizeable raise and a lot of credit because I had intuition superior to others."

When would he turn over his findings to authorities prior to publishing an investigative story?

"If I had knowledge of a crime ... I think I would divulge information—something I know—if it would prove the innocence or guilt of someone involved in the crime. If somebody called me tomorrow night and told me of a murder plot I think it would be my duty as a private citizen to call the police or the district attorney to tell them what I know of this and explain the details," Peter suggests, adding that he believes the responsibility of citizenship includes such action. "Where my responsibilities as a newsman would begin is if I were asked where I got the information, I would act on the presumption that (1) the person who called me could have just as easily called the police and (2) he is probably not the perpetrator because if he were he would want the plot to be successful and therefore wouldn't have called anyone in the first place. Thus, I wouldn't divulge any information about my source ... and I don't happen to believe that to have knowledge of a crime necessarily means I'm an accessory to it."

While he knows his answer does not win friends among law enforcement officials and law-and-order citizenry, memories of his own court fight are too recent to put aside. He can well remember how alone he felt the day the handcuffs were locked on his wrists and he was led to the lockup because of his refusal to divulge information. There wasn't a reporter in the courtroom. And he was bitterly disappointed.

"I'm not an exhibitionist and I don't need an audience. But the lack of one that day caused me for the first time to examine my actions. I had considered myself as a kind of surrogate of the press during the unfolding of the case. . . . Even though I could easily justify my stand on a personal ethical level, I preferred the higher ground of professional integrity and the public right to a free flow of information. If I had buckled in my resolve, I would have run the danger of destroying sources for newspeople all over the country. By standing fast, I believe, I have not only helped preserve those sources, but possibly even strengthened them. In responding that way, I believe I was doing nothing more or less than any reporter would do. These were some of my thoughts during my three-hour stay (September 27, 1973) the first time I was put in that jail cell."

And those thoughts were extremely important to Peter. They probably kept him from seeking other employment even though job opportunities, which appeared good at the time, evaporated when he was released. "That experience has done me little good, at least insofar as employment and income are concerned. People who might have considered me in the past don't really want anything to do with me now because of my irreverence. But I'm only mildly annoyed by that because my intuition told me it would be this way. . . .It is not difficult for me to continue my love affair with reporting because it is one profession that seems to like me. Furthermore, it is still one of the last refuges for the truth. Going to jail, I discovered, was no more than my rather outspoken way of paying my dues. The news business has been good to me for more than a decade, so one small aberration in all of that time can hardly be cause to blacken the whole profession. Besides, it was not the newspaper business that caused me to go to jail. It was a very political lawyer who happened to be the prosecutor. I don't think I will ever practice law because of that experience."

But he doesn't believe his actions should be interpreted as the beginning of the era of militancy among young reporters. He believes, quite to the contrary, beginners don't take the time to understand thoroughly the news business. "You really need a year to hone your skills and become thoroughly familiar. After that, you should be looking for a place where you can be valuable. Some people remain reporters all their lives; others take a liking to desk work; still others prefer to become administrators. I've done all three and found reporting most satisfying to me. The attitude should be that a newsman or person is working for the public, not himself. His dedication should be truth, not aggrandizement, and his product should be in a state of constant improvement."

More important, he points out, those who plan to enter the field should be more realistic about assessing it. "On a scale of one to ten, I would say the job the media do in informing the public is about seven on the average. There is a terrible herd of sacred cows in some parts of media and there are faint hearts in others. There are papers and television and radio stations that are doing a job worth a ten rating—the tops—and others that obviously do a one job. But that is because the press in this country is free. A free press comes in two forms—good and bad. A controlled press comes in only one variety—bad. As I sat in that jailhouse, the public outrage literally radiated through the walls. That pleased me a great deal. The response . . . restored a faltering faith that any action would occur. I seriously wondered if I wanted to continue in a profession that was too fat and lazy to defend itself against a dangerous attack. I decided to stay because I love it and there is still hope."

The decision was not easy though. Life as a reporter has interfered with personal and family plans as well as goals of a more comfortable life. "Frankly, landing in the clink for twenty days was the wrong thing at the wrong time. My wife was within days of delivering our third child. A year-long strike (1971–72) at the *News* had drained our resources dry, meager as they were to begin with. No publisher would take on a reporter who brought with him potential legal fees and costs running into the thousands. While I would react exactly the same way today as I did then to the prosecutor's demands, I wish the whole thing had happened at some other time. But the fact of the adversity of the time and my own actions serves to underline that the logical solution, as usual, did not appeal to me. Rather, it was the intuitive reaction that prevailed. I survived and I sleep at night, poor but reverent with self-satisfaction.

"I may very well be sick in the head, because my attitude has sometimes brought me right up to the brink of disaster and my family right along with me. Before I landed my present job, for example, with the *National Star* as an investigative reporter I had $250 in a bank account and thirteen cents in my pocket. I relied upon my intuitive feeling that things would happen before we went down the drain. And it did. I'm working . . . doing the kind of work I know best, do best, and certainly enjoy best. My intuition tells me there are bigger and better things for me in the future.

"I have very few friends because I define the term severely. I don't necessarily strive for upward mobility because I feel that professionally I am in the top ranks, and personally I am such a self-confident middle-class slob that there is no hope for me. I watch the Peter Principle operate effectively all around me, confident in the thought that if I ever yielded to it I would rise to the position of publisher somewhere and would profoundly be incompetent in such a spot."

His definition of a friend is akin to his explanation of family. "We invite people into our home who accept us, and we don't worry about those who don't. It's their loss, not ours. Nobody who enters our home is ever insulted here and believe me, we've had some weirdos. We expect the same wherever we go. We travel in a tight circle of acquaintances that is diverse. I hang out with colleagues myself, but the family circle is diverse enough that everyone can talk with everyone else without being shut out or bored. I have sometimes been sorely disappointed by those who would be my 'friends' but never by those who are my family. . . . We enjoy being together for no other reason than companionship. I often go fishing with my son; I watch a girls' softball game, not for love of the game, but because my daughter's playing. My personal, off-the-job life is normally a style by committee, since it revolves around my family. We talk about everything, even though my wife would prefer some subjects to be reserved for a conversation without children. But they have to learn, and God put us on earth to teach them, I believe. The most powerful teacher is example, and we have a lot of good to pack into our example. Frankness, openness, truthfulness are all important to that example. I don't fear that my children will ever find it impossible to discuss their problems or their joys with us."

A glance at the photograph of his wife and kids answering questions gives Peter a chance to reflect.

"I personally gave up a long time ago trying to be anyone but myself, which is to say a rather lazy individual who was fortunate enough to fall into a line of work that he likes and to which he is able to devote considerable time and energy. Rather than try to be like others—although there are many I admire—I try not to be like many writers and reporters whom I know because some are much less than they appear to be."

Photo of Larry Brinton courtesy of the Nashville *Banner,*
Owen Cartwright, photographer.

5

Investigative Stories Come in All Sizes for Larry Brinton

It doesn't take much of an investigation to give Nashville *Banner* investigative reporter Larry Brinton satisfaction.

"Not long ago I tracked down a dognapper who had stolen a French poodle from a parked car. The fact that the dognapper was going on trial for first-degree murder within two weeks and that juries would not look favorably on someone who would steal a pet resulted in getting the dog back for its owners. May not sound like the kind of thing an investigative reporter should spend his time on but it was a good feeling for me," Larry says with a trace of a smile. "The happiness in the eyes of the owners made my effort really worthwhile." And you know he means it.

It's worthwhile, he continues, when you solve any case. "Actually I enjoy my work now as an investigative reporter just like I did the almost fourteen years I spent as a crime reporter. It takes initiative to do both jobs, along with a lot of curiosity and suspicion as to why things are like they are or appear to be. Since junior high school days I wanted to be a reporter and I have the same feeling of excitement about being a reporter today as I had when I started twenty years ago."

Forty-four-year-old Brinton is a home-grown product, educated in Nashville's public schools and Peabody College. He left the city once to spend four years in the navy.

After his discharge, it was back to the seat and shrine of country music. He joined the *Banner* staff in 1955 on the state news desk. He moved to police and criminal courts for a decade and a half, created the *Banner*'s first consumer protection column called Help Desk, and served for a short time as assistant city editor. His contacts in the city and the state and his experiences made him a logical choice by management when the Gannett Group decided the *Banner* needed a full-time investigative reporter.

Some outstanding reporters have preceded him in Nashville. The *Banner* 's sister paper, the larger morning daily, the *Tennessean,* featured the work of John Seigenthaler (now publisher) on a variety of local and state issues. "Seigenthaler," said Clark Mollenhoff, a veteran investigative reporter and dean of the Washington press corps, "is one of the real pros in this business. His work provided valuable insights into investigative reporting in the South."

But Larry Brinton proved the *Banner* management knew its business, too. It also proved that investigative reporting in responsible hands does not have to look far for issues. In fact, local stories handled by a good reporter with probing questions can achieve the same recognition as an investigation in a major metropolitan area such as Boston, Philadelphia, New York . . . even Washington.

Several *Banner* investigations by Brinton were carried by the wire services and major newspapers nationally and internationally. In December 1972, for example, it was Larry's stories that first revealed how a debt-ridden Nashvillian was jailed—the first U.S. citizen named in a conspiracy to assassinate Philippines President Ferdinand E. Marcos. Manila newspapers later quoted Brinton and the *Banner* story as the source for the identity of the man.

A more satisfying investigation, Larry says, was his examination of the United Cerebral Palsy program and its use of gifts and donations in Nashville. "There was real personal satisfaction in exposing it. It resulted in multiple felony charges of larceny being lodged against the UCP officials. More important, state and city laws were rewritten to strengthen present statutes concerning the solicitation of funds for charities as a result of the investigation," he adds with a degree of pride.

Twenty years as a reporter told him something was wrong—terribly wrong—with the way the United Cerebral Palsy funds were being tossed about by the Middle Tennessee chapter in Nashville. He remembers it was on a very cold day in February that he was sure that he had solid data to pursue his investigation. He felt, after days of telephone calls and attempts to meet and talk with UCP officials, that he simply wasn't getting straight answers about how the money was disbursed.

The tip about the story had come innocently enough. In an effort to support the UCP and a local telethon to raise money for the organization, *Lifestyles* reporter Phyllis White had been assigned to do a feature on one hundred children at one of the centers. While talking to the executive director of the organization she was told that, although the previous year's telethon had raised $276,981 in pledges and gifts, the program was nearly broke. The casual comment disturbed Ms. White. To Brinton, it was a starting point.

During the days that followed he gathered bits and

pieces. Then he was ready to have a look at UCP records. Organization officials ignored his first requests and refused to supply much of the information he asked for. Consequently, Brinton enlisted the aid of *Banner* Publisher Wayne Sargent, Editor Ken Morrell, and former Special Watergate Prosecutor James F. Neal, the *Banner*'s legal counsel, to gain access to the charity's financial records and other data.

Within weeks, Brinton could have published the first of his subsequent series of twenty-five stories, well in advance of the organization's telecast soliciting funds. But a decision was made to wait until after the television benefit was held.

"The major significance . . . was that I knew in advance of publication that many people, including the palsied children, would be hurt as a result of the stories. This included UCP staff members, directors, their families, and other charities desperately needing funds for continuation of their operations. I also felt that by exposing the wrongs of UCP management, the benefits of the investigation would come to the palsied children by way of restoring new confidence in contributors who would know that their donations would be spent for what they had been contributed, this being the children afflicted with palsy."

The president of the television station, WSM-TV, Nashville, attended one of the meetings where newspaper officials were challenging UCP officials' right to withhold records. The organization's refusal left a lasting impression. Days later, the station, which had donated free time to the charity, cancelled the telethon forty-eight hours before it was scheduled to be broadcast. The same day, Brinton's series unfolded telling Nashville residents:

* Advance salaries to at least three employes over a number of years were never repaid;

* A new auto was purchased for the executive director's personal use in 1972 from UCP funds;
* Donations were used to purchase whiskey and perfume for visiting telethon stars along with jewelry and gifts for staff members and some officers;
* Thirty-two different bank accounts, both saving and checking, were uncovered although UCP accountants knew of only a few;
* Top staff employees were drawing additional salaries under such categories and budget titles as "program services" and "patient applicants" in addition to unsubstantiated trips;
* Financial reports were only hypothetical figures to show how monies should have been spent, not how monies were actually handled;
* The chapter owed the national UCP organization more than $80,000.

Larry had spent most of the month on the story and had sketched a picture which revealed only a small percentage of actual donations going to cerebral palsy victims. And he still had only limited access to UCP records.

The series had the kind of repercussions that might have caused others to back away. "I really got to the point where I actually didn't know what to expect next," he told his editor one day when it was obvious that UCP had also paid members of the media—some of his own friends—to serve as consultants. Among those discovered on the UCP payroll were a *Banner* senior editor who received $4,300 over a period of several years and a photographer who freelanced for the charity. Larry's article on media was a front-page story complete with information about the *Banner* employees involved. The editor returned the money voluntarily and admitted his error in judgment.

While the work demanded guts, it also took stamina.

"My work day normally starts at 7:00 A.M. and during an investigation like that one there's no telling when it ends. The UCP work took Saturdays and Sundays and weekday nights. The days would include discussing fresh information or details with editors and/or the publisher or the actual writing of the stories. In between all of that, of course, there were scores of telephone calls to take and make concerning the investigation. And there were calls about other cases that I was stringing along while I worked on UCP.

"And you can't just change the scenery by going home to stop the phone calls either. They continue because an investigative reporter must stay on top of the city happenings at all times—not just when you're on duty or in the city room."

It was just such a call that came to Brinton as he wrapped up the UCP case that led to an investigation into the Disabled American Veterans' sponsorship of a thrift store that was actually owned by a California management firm. And, while sources and documents were again scarce, Larry persisted to get piece after piece of the story. Local and state DAV officers and the California firm refused to provide details, so Brinton went to see national leaders in Cincinnati. They called a special meeting to hear his views about the store.

The peripatetic investigator, his editor along to help out, told DAV officials that in Nashville alone the organization received only $15,600 in a three-and-a-half-year period while the store grossed $785,000 in sales. The Nashville public was being deceived, he insisted, by contributing clothing, furniture, and other items for the benefit of the veterans when only 2 percent gross sales actually went to the DAV.

His information was most convincing. The executive committee of the national DAV canceled its contract in

Nashville and thirty-four other thrift stores from Florida to California.

To Larry, that's where the real satisfaction is. It's the kind of work where the results of each case compensate for long hours and a great many frustrations. "About four years ago I was 'promoted' to the city desk," he laughs. "It took me almost eighteen months to get back to writing. Since there are not big amounts of money for either reporters or editors, except in rare occasions, then a person should try to do what he likes to do best and what he can do best. A good reporter, whether investigative or general assignment, has more power and prestige than most editors and many times, makes more money than editors other than the top editor or two of a newspaper. My salary is more than most editors' on this paper and just slightly behind that of the managing editor. I'm doing what I like and I intend to stay at it."

Unlike others in the field, Larry keeps his wife and two sons in the dark most of the time about his work. "I only talk in general terms on stories with my wife and there are many aspects of investigations which she reads in the *Banner* just the same as any other subscriber. When a reporter is working day and night, not merely on a particular investigation, he hardly has the time to explain fully all of the details to his family, although family members can understand many points of the story from the many telephone conversations if they want to, I suppose."

But even an alert family member would have trouble keeping track of Larry's investigations—those already in print and those still in process—and his sources. A few years ago, he obtained the contents of a tape recording between FBI agents at the Jacksonville, Florida, airport tower and the pilot of a hijacked plane the bureau was trying to rescue. It was Brinton who found the late country music star Stringbean Akeman's handbag with $3,000 in canceled checks while police worked round the clock to find evidence in the murder of the entertainer and his wife outside their secluded Nashville home. He is also credited by police officers as the person who obtained a detailed confession from one of the killers.

"I'm a loner, a maverick, or whatever you want to call it. That's been most successful for me," he says without hesitation. "There are not many other reporters on this newspaper, though, who would go for this line of work. It takes a lot of dedication, hard work, patient building of good informants, etc., and many reporters simply aren't willing to do it. I am. However, I'm a loner because that's the way I want it."

Shield laws, he insists, are helpful; "they just don't go far enough. I'm involved in a litigation in which my editor, myself, and another reporter have refused to divulge the source of two stories written by the other reporter and me. The suit was originally brought by a former Memphis judge who was a candidate for nomination by the Democratic Executive Committee for a Supreme Court post in Tennessee. He claimed the stories hurt his chances and he brought suit against the executive committee, trying to use us as witnesses.

"When a Shelby Court upheld our right against disclosure, the judge's attorney then brought a $500,000 libel suit against the newspaper. Since the shield law does not extend to libel suits, it is the contention of the plaintiff judge and his lawyer that we will have to reveal our sources. Our lawyer contends the action in bringing the libel suit was done to circumvent the shield law ruling in the initial suit against the executive committee. A shield law, in other words, doesn't really give you protection if the plaintiff wants to find other ways to get your sources made public in court."

There are other hassles, too. In Larry's opinion, most of them occur while the reporter is trying to gain a person's confidence to get information. "The worst problem, I believe, is that of telephoning someone for information who is in an official capacity. Most people are immediately defensive as soon as you tell them who you are. There is also a hassle in trying to carry out an investigation and, at the same time, keep it low-key enough that the competition—The *Tennessean*—doesn't learn what you're doing before you get it into print."

But the problems are manageable. "They're really annoyances. I can't say that I really dislike any part of my job because all of it is a challenge and that's what it's all about. That may sound hoky to some but that's how I feel. Many reporters are neither skilled or dedicated enough to do this type of work, nor are they prepared to spend the time it takes in developing contacts or informants. It's easier for them to do the puff stories, make the press parties, and try not to offend."

There are no puff stories in Larry Brinton's file, though, friends say.

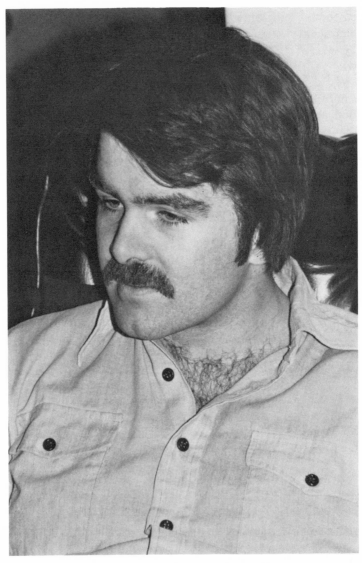

Photo of K. Scott Christianson by John Tibbetts.

6

K. Scott Christianson: The Man Albany Remembers

Albany, New York, will long remember K. Scott Christianson. The Albany Police Department, however, would like to forget him. K. Scott Christianson is a muckraker who has sometimes been called an investigative reporter.

"I prefer the term 'muckraking' despite the fact that 'investigative reporting' is in vogue and although the former carries a rather sensational connotation for some people," he says. "I do not believe the muckrakers should serve the same function as cops or DAs or that they should employ the same tactics. Investigative reporting conjures up all kinds of police images for me, which I find extremely distasteful, and muckraking, on the other hand, has historically been closely associated with the Left, and with those of a more philosophical bent who have sought to alter the existing order—to change the system."

Enter the Albany Police Department.

During the summer of 1971, Scott, then an investigative reporter for Bob Fichenberg's Albany *Knickerbocker News,* launched an intensive examination of area law enforcement. He gathered so much material, in fact, that he voluntarily went to state investigators and asked them to look into the situation. Using a mysterious "J," a major heroin pusher, as a primary source, Scott compiled information from nearly three hundred police experts, beat cops, drug specialists, community leaders, priests, doctors, junkies, victims, prostitutes, and others.

"What this newspaper found with their help," he wrote, "(is) a story of a multimillion-dollar enterprise that involves hundreds of perpetrators and thousands of victims each day; a tragic condition that has killed some young people and ruined others; a gnawing problem that is eroding many residents' faith in the entire criminal justice system."

In a series of nine dialogue-filled, fact-packed articles during the final week of October 1971, Christianson raked political leaders, cops, and others and exploded the abuses. A sensitive subject, especially to Albany policemen. "At a time when law enforcement in general is under heavy fire, dishonesty, greed, and ruthlessness in the Albany Police Department are fostering deep distrust and disgust. The result: many residents have simply given up trying to help police catch criminals," he charged on October 26 in an article entitled "Albany Police Corruption Flourishes."

Unlike some of his investigative counterparts, Scott tried to provide the reader with solutions to the problem. In assessing the impact of growing corruption, he warned Albanyites: "Most importantly, public confidence in their police must be restored. Public informants cannot be ignored, frightened away, or betrayed by crooked cops. Residents must feel safe, should they elect to furnish information about drug pushers, pimps, and other criminals.

Coordination between city, state, and federal law enforcement agencies—which is now literally nonexistent in drug
and vice cases—must be established. But even the most
thorough housecleaning of the Albany Police Department
would not necessarily shut down the city's booming dope
and prostitution rackets. Rehabilitation must be acceler-
ated, intensified, and supported. Addict treatment programs, drug referral agencies, health clinics, and jails and
prisons must be improved. The rate of recidivism for
addicts and criminals is abysmally poor, for the system
tends to reinforce these tendencies, not eliminate them."

His charges brought swift reactions. Albany Mayor,
sixty-four-year-old Erastus Corning II, while calling the
News charges "completely irresponsible," promised to investigate. The State Commission of Investigation, which
had already been conducting informal discussions on the
subject, and the Albany County District Attorney initiated probes. And Editor Fichenberg refused to let glib
political figures muscle in on Christianson's work. Said
the editor: "Our man Christianson has put too much of
himself, too much hard digging, sweat, grit, determination, and courage for his efforts to be belittled and under-
cut at this stage, through implication, by any public official who is concerned about what this series may have
done to his public image. And we're not about to let anyone get away with it."

The blockbusting stories produced months of hearings, allegations, and threats. The threats reached the
young reporter, his wife Kathleen, and their two kids,
Kelly and Emily. "I try to keep my family as separate
from my work as I can, though this has never really been
possible. While working on a number of projects, I've had
to send my family away—to relatives or a hotel—for
their own safety. My wife has also had to put up with
much of the aggravation that has gone with my work—
phone calls at 4 A.M., threats, harassment, tax audit, etc."

And there were times when the investigation, regardless of how well it was documented and executed, proved nothing. It happened in Albany.

"In retrospect, the newspaper probe and the two-year state investigation it set in motion appear to have resulted in little significant improvement of the Albany police. Indeed, the whole affair may even have backfired against the department's critics. . . . Many of its recent witnesses now find it extremely hard to get employment, and some have suffered permanent disgrace for what they said. . . . Meanwhile, the police department continues to operate as it always has done. Its ranks remain intact, no commanders have been replaced. All of the remaining officers who figured prominently in the corruption charges continue on duty and some have even gained promotions," he told readers of *The Nation,* December 3, 1973.

A similar kind of exasperation with local law enforcement months later caused the young muckraker to react indignantly to a perfunctory press release about a hanging in the Albany County Jail. He took the announcement apart word for word and, after an intensive investigation, wrote a penetrating article for *The Washington Park Spirit* (an alternative news biweekly in Albany which folded in early 1975) about the system's careless indifference to the final days and subsequent jailhouse death of a bright southern black (*magna cum laude* from Dillard with a master's from Brown) named Leonard Smith, the circumstances that surrounded his apparent suicide and the people Scott held responsible, in part, for it. His two-and-a-half tabloid page story was persuasive. It attacked institutions, systems, and people; took the reader inside the jail and the insidious politics of the system; and reconstructed the dead man's last days and hours.

"As so often happens, those who'd known the dead man grieved over him and felt guilty," Scott wrote.

"Those with good reason to feel responsible felt threatened, shedding sweat, not tears.

"In the ensuing press coverage, the local news media seized upon Smith as a newsworthy statistic who would make some good copy. He was the fourth inmate suicide at the jail in less than a year.... Smith had had 'mental problems' so he probably should not have been in jail at all. Bureaucratic red tape had delayed his transfer to a psychiatric hospital.

"The story seemed to fit neatly into current events. It might lend a decent balance to the coverage of the Garrow trial (a murder trial then in progress in upstate New York), since both involved alleged criminals with head problems. Best of all, it got the jail back on page one—and in a way which was sure to strike political sparks. Send a photographer out to get some human interest pictures of his grieving family, and a reporter to find out who to blame for this mess.

"But much of what the media reported was inaccurate and fragmentary. Lenny Smith didn't kill himself and no one individual could take the whole rap for his death. He did not die quickly or unexpectedly, but rather, his demise was slow and agonizing, tragic and embittering. Unusual, yet typical.

"Before Leonard Smith's heart stopped beating and his brain suffered its last painful memory, he had run a long and battering gauntlet all alone—an experience so horrifying that the terrors of life finally outweighed the terrors of death. From a tiny Louisiana hamlet peopled with cheerful black faces, an extraordinary man had developed, only to face stern white faces. That man had excelled at every stage of his long and tortuous climb to success until suddenly, at the brink of his uppermost reaches, something happened. The manchild in the promised land found it hell. His grip loosened. And he fell.

"At the State Office Campus [where he worked] he

was made a prisoner in Building 1, then transferred to Cell 2 in the county jail. There, he finally smoked his last cigarette. And [he] was hanged. This is Lenny Smith's story. Though he can't talk, he must scream. It is also the story of his killers. Though they should talk, they stay silent."

Lenny's crime, Scott continued, was a fight he had with an office supervisor. It started with words in the hall and ended moments later after the enraged black man had struck his office colleague several times with a stick. The reason for the fight? Smith had been fired and lost an appeal to return to work. Months before, his application for a federal fellowship had been rejected. The supervisor, Lenny believed, had been instrumental in each of these setbacks.

But the system and its agents, Scott wrote, reacted without a trace of compassion. "The police located Smith and he was placed under arrest on a charge of second degree assault, a Class D felony punishable by a maximum prison term of seven years. The most generous assessment of such a charge for such an act is that it was excessive—second degree assault is one which must result in serious physical injury which may be likely to cause death or permanent serious disfigurement. A more realistic description of the charge is that it was unsupportable by the evidence and that it betrayed a we'll-fix-him attitude which smacked of unmitigated callousness and racism."

Confinement, his legal defense, meetings with psychiatrists and court sessions entangled Leonard Smith in a hopeless one-hundred-fourteen-day ordeal for which he could see only one solution: death. Yet even his decision to save himself from the complexities of life ended in confusion and controversy, Scott told his readers. "Smith was taken down and beaten on the chest. He was rushed

downstairs to the nurse. The ambulance was called....
The medical care Smith received has not been verified.
...Since no doctor was in the jail at the time—only a
doctor can legally determine death—Lenny Smith may
still have been alive, though if he was, his brain had
probably been destroyed by the ordeal." What has been
verified is that a rescue squad from a nearby village
arrived shortly after the call was placed, Scott says.

But a mysterious twenty-minute delay in the life-
saving drama that took place in the jail puzzles the reporter. There are too many explanations needed, Scott
charges, concluding that "Smith was murdered. Murdered by dozens of authorities in dozens of ways. Again
and again. They murdered him."

But that's the kind of frustration twenty-eight-
year-old Scott Christianson has risked since he became
a journalist in 1965 when he joined the college newspaper
at the University of Connecticut. "I was an English major actually—American history and journalism minor.
I had been on the high school paper along with the student council, varsity football, track, and wrestling. But
in college I also tried a number of journalistic jobs to
gain experience and to work my way through school: I
was a public relations writer for the university—I was
always somewhat shocked that so many newspapers published my press releases verbatim, often with a byline—
assistant to the head of the journalism department where
I edited an interdisciplinary weekly called 'The 30's
Times,' editor of a number of weekly and annual sheets
and a campus stringer for the Hartford *Courant*. I took
everything and anything really to support my college education from June 1965, to the summer of 1969. I paid 60
percent of all my costs by working as a theater manager,
lifeguard, housepainter, cook, and resident adviser at the
university at the same time.

"After graduation, I chose between two alternatives: work for a medium-sized newspaper long enough to learn the ropes and gain some credits or start at the bottom on a larger paper with the slim hope of some day winning a worthwhile position. I took the former route and I've never regretted it. Nor have I regretted avoiding journalism school, either at the undergraduate or graduate level."

He joined the Knickerbocker *News* in June 1969, and for the first few months, he wondered if he had made a mistake. "I tried my hand at a number of dull tasks. I started as a copy editor, then was elevated to assistant to the editor of the editorial page, before being made co-editor of the weekly tabloid, and later, suburban reporter and general assignment reporter. It proved to be an educational apprenticeship, since I got a taste of virtually every phase of editorial production. My first news story at the Knick turned out to be a fairly successful crusade on the subject of low-income housing. After a time, I was made a full-time investigative reporter.

"It was an exciting time to be a newspaperman and I was glad by then to have chosen Albany. In addition to being the capital city, its style of local government was a wonder to behold—as many know, Albany has one of the oldest old-style political machines in the country and there was never a shortage of shit to uncover. Rocky [Nelson Rockefeller, former governor] was in Albany and his tomb—the South Mall [a state building project started by the Rockefeller Administration]. I learned a lot about the workings of government and saw the way the system worked to screw the little people. It was a time of great confrontations, and Albany was the scene of many marches, sit-ins, and so on; the hard hat was a national symbol at the time and Albany was the site of the largest construction project in the country (the

Mall). I was a reporter when men landed on the moon and the war was the source of discontent."

His job has changed frequently during the past decade, though. He left the Knickerbocker *News* during the summer of 1972 and returned to the university—the State University of New York's School of Criminal Justice in Albany—where he completed work on a master's in 1973 and continued for his doctorate. Yet, academic pursuits didn't affect his interest in investigative work and writing. Actually, they became more interwoven. "I'm working full-time as a researcher on alternatives to prison, a one-year policy study funded by the state university. I'm a project coordinator involved in all phases, data gathering, analysis, literature research, evaluation, and the writing of preliminary and final reports. I co-host a weekly radio show, occasionally serve as an interviewer on television shows, I edited a book on criminal justice, and I'm writing a book, writing a dissertation, and generally working my ass off. I was an investigative reporter and political writer for the *Washington Park Spirit*, Albany's biweekly alternative paper, until it folded. It was considerably left of the Hearst paper I started with.

"And I still lecture frequently about muckraking. I have appeared in over fifty engagements ranging from law schools to service clubs, TV and radio to high schools and grade schools. But it's very difficult for me to state my philosophy of muckraking or to dredge up war stories at my tender age. . . . I've accumulated a few, though."

While his peer group attempts to find security in fraternities, clubs, and associations, Scott takes a different approach. "I'm a loner, of course, I'm not the type to fraternize much," says the one-time fraternity president and class vice president. "I would say he's a very intense person," says a former newspaper associate. And, unlike others his age who hold names such as Jack Anderson,

Clark Mollenhoff, and Bill Lambert in awe, he sets his own goals.

"I remain troubled over the fact that most so-called investigative reporters (Anderson, Bob Greene of *Newsday*, Nick Gage of the New York *Times*) serve as arms for the police and for those in power, that they continue to churn out simplistic stuff about the evils of 'organized crime' and so on, without going after more fundamental things. For my money, the best muckrakers around today are Sy Hersh and Jack Nelson, not necessarily in that order. I also admire fine writing and to my way of thinking the most outstanding piece of muckraking I've seen in recent years in article form—there are many fine books on it—has been 'Death in the Wilderness: The Justice Department's Killer Nark Strike Force' by Joe Eszterhas (*Rolling Stone*, May 24, 1973).

"What sets today's investigative reporting apart from earlier eras of muckraking is not its spirit, for both are unmistakably geared to achieve reform. Rather, it has only been within the last few years that this new creature has emerged—that a specialty has been made of it," Christianson wrote in a *Quill* article several years ago. "Investigative reporters armed with new techniques, now are seeking to make an art of muckraking—one which will enable it to endure. They have begun, like Philip Meyer of Knight Newspapers, to use computers and mathematical formulae—to harness new energy. They have probed the pollution of environment and explored new ways to help the consumer. . . . An investigative reporter is not a cop out. He is not a subversive. He is willing to work within the system to expose the system to improve the system. Perhaps he can only say with some certainty 'I tried.' "

When investigative reporting is conscientious, authentic, and strives, above all, for accuracy, he says, it makes great strides in communities, states, and in the nation. Reporters have solved murders, cleared innocent people, and introduced much-needed legislation.

Having authentic, documented stories, though, doesn't guarantee publication. "Getting the story can be rough, but getting it published can be rougher," he claims. "Unlike most reporters, the investigative newsman must constantly do battle with the company lawyers and the whole gamut of editors, all of whom do their best to challenge every word. There are times when compromises have to be made, but there are also times when every good man must fight tooth and nail for his story. Sometimes the watchful eyes are only testing; sometimes they are merely seeking new ways to rise up the corporate pecking order."

Some ambitious newspaperpersons may accept the corporate concept of money, power, and prestige with position; Scott can't. "It doesn't compare at all with my goals and I don't agree that most journalists aspire to be editors and certainly not most investigative reporters. On the contrary, the investigative reporters I have known choose as their primary targets those with money, prestige, and power."

His essay on Representative Sam Stratton of New York's Schenectady district for the *Park Spirit* is an example of how he picks his targets. Depicting Stratton as a military establishment type who reaps political benefits, Scott wrote: "Sam Stratton is many things, but he is not merely Sam Stratton. To understand him, it is necessary to examine the city—Schenectady—where he grew up, worked, and emerged as a political power.... Sam Stratton is General Electric Sam Stratton, Schenectady is a GE town.... [It] runs a good part of the world. All three are plugged into each other through a complex maze of circuits, wires, and outlets, like some enormous switchboard. The difference, of course, is that the city and the congressman need the company to survive, whereas GE could flip the switch at any moment without receiving so much as a shock, for it owns dozens of other cities and politicians who could take their place at the drop of a memo."

Investigative reporting, he insists, involves much more than "the romanticized horse manure that is written by hot shot newspaper sleuths. It's been my experience that investigative reporting often results in a situation that is either no better, or worse, than that which exists prior to the noble effort. It is very, very rare that even the finest projects drastically improve matters. The reporter's key sources, who often cooperate with him out of sincere outrage or disillusionment at what they have witnessed, are very often destroyed in the wake of the story; if they are lucky, they escape with only minor scars, bruises, and bitterness. Management really doesn't give a shit about important investigative reporting, and when put to the test, they will usually act in much the same way as cornered rats whose only wish is to protect themselves, and their nests, as well as their profits."

The Albany muckraker, who was born in Boston and grew up in the suburban New York capital district of Delmar, has no illusions about the current popularity of investigative journalism. "Investigative reporting is approaching the end of another golden period," he maintains. "For a number of economic reasons, it will soon begin to enter—if it hasn't already—a period of sharp decline. Today, every burnt-out, apathetic punk who is fresh out of J-school, wants to be a hot shot investigative reporter. Management will exploit this and exploit them. There will be less boat rocking, and because of the shortage of jobs, young reporters will do what management wants them to do, which is to increase profits. And to hell with social improvements, righting wrongs, and so on."

In his opinion, the situation cannot be avoided. Newspapers operate in a way similar to the corporate structure that was openly attacked in the late 1960s. As corporations, newspapers attract corporate executives who make "corporate" kinds of decisions. "I was constantly amused by the position of (newspaper) management during the great debate over newsmen's privilege. Whenever a reporter is subpoenaed in a criminal case, and forced to disclose his sources or go to jail—depending on whether or not there's a shield law—management will scream in protest. 'A blow to freedom of the press,' the editorial writers invariably proclaim. But in a civil case, when the newspaper's money is at stake, management couldn't care less about the inviolability of newsmen's privilege. In such situations, reporters generally are expected to throw in their sources, in order to protect the company's interest."

How can investigative reporting be improved?

By refocusing on topics of real concern and being more selective about who practices it. "Investigative reportage is usually directed against the wrong targets," Scott charges. "It looks at the Mafia hoods rather than the corporate ones. Most investigative stuff is also terribly lifeless and dull. Superficial. It lacks analysis. It could happen because of reporter ineptness, pressures to write a so-called investigative story on a popular subject, pressures to get it in print, or merely lousy editing among other things. Then, too, investigative reporters have to assume responsibility for their work. Since most of what they do is doomed to fizzle or backfire, they owe it to their sources and to others who take risks in order to help, to protect them from total destruction."

And what of Scott Christianson's future?

While he's accumulated newspaper awards—Hearst National Writing Competition and Empire State Chapter of Sigma Delta Chi among others—and he's been nominated for a Pulitzer Prize and national Sigma Delta Chi recognition, Scott's plans don't include daily journalism. He may write an occasional piece for contemporary periodicals—the *Village Voice,* the *Nation,* publications he's written for during recent years—but he has other plans for the decade ahead.

"Eventually, I plan to write novels—indeed, that's what I sought to prepare myself for when I entered the newspaper racket, ten years ago."

Photo of Gene Cunningham by Joel Barkin.

7

Gene Cunningham Believes Investigative Reporters Can Be Gregarious, Too

For twenty days, a young reporter named Stuart Wilk received vouchers, checks, and bus tickets amounting to $145.20 from the Milwaukee County Welfare Department.

It was easy, he said. He walked in off the street in casual clothes and a beard of several days' growth, filled out the forms, and walked out and waited for the money to come. And nobody checked his application.

That's the way Wilk and veteran investigative reporter Gene Cunningham got at the truth of the allegations of fraud, waste, and mismanagement in the county welfare system. Their employer, the Milwaukee *Sentinel,* gave the results of the three-month investigation front page treatment for days. The series laid bare what many had suspected; some citizens of Milwaukee County were receiving help they weren't entitled to.

Worse, though, was the apathy the welfare department showed in grasping the situation. Nearly everything he filled out on the forms, Wilk said, was untrue. Had the department attempted to verify the application, it would have found him ineligible for general relief. He used a borrowed Social Security card as identification although such cards clearly state they are for Social Security and tax purposes. And he rented a room in a boarding house that he didn't use; he merely chatted with the landlord a few times. Even after Wilk's case was identified as fictitious, he was routinely given the opportunity to appeal and possibly get back on the welfare roster.

But that wasn't all. The two reporters' sources helped them construct specific instances where double checks were issued to recipients; duplicate payments were made to cover welfare clients' bills; food stamps and bus passes were sold for drinking money; exaggerated mileage vouchers and overtime were charged to the department; employes admitted taking working hours off; and in one case, three refrigerators were actually given to one recipient in less than four months.

Welfare checks, they further discovered, were sent to such places as taverns; rent deposits were paid to clients in condemned housing; housing inspectors "inspected" buildings by telephone and checks were occasionally made out to persons with two or three aliases.

The *Sentinel* series showed as much as 20 percent fraud and administrative error involved in the scandal, amounting to an estimated $28 million in one year alone.

It did bring action, though. The county board's Welfare and Human Resources Committee began an investigation based upon the articles and a subcommittee of the state legislature launched a study of the problem. A statewide examination of welfare operations was urged by one state senator and legislation was introduced to tighten employee supervision in welfare departments throughout the state.

Meanwhile, the *Sentinel's* exposé brought accolades from readers and leaders (the governor termed the stories "a fine piece of reporting").

But it was all in a day's work for Gene. She had pried open such wormy subjects as gambling, organized crime, conditions in nursing homes, and the activities of a county board chairman since she joined the Milwaukee morning daily. And her work had brought formal investigations before, too. In some cases, it led to the elimination of wrongdoers and doings.

"I have some *very* strong feelings about journalism and investigative reporting. They come from long years at this and from bumping into all kinds and types of assignments, most of which I suggested myself," she contends. "The *Sentinel* has been into investigative reporting for many years and prides itself on what has been accomplished as a result. I'm happy to be in the middle of it and more than happy to work for a newspaper that sees investigative reporting as the important facet of journalism it really is."

Facts support what she says, too.

Ten years ago the *Sentinel* boasted it would be an action paper; one that devotes its resources to the public interest. It has made progress in meeting the claim. An eight-month investigation of commercial gambling, for example, resulted in fines and jail terms for seven men. A series on nursing home abuses in the state attracted legislative interest and brought new rules and improvements in conditions and supervision in the homes. In 1974, a series on conditions in the Milwaukee County Health Center initiated a broad-based probe by a task force of the Mental Health Planning Committee and much of the *Sentinel's* arguments and research were substantiated by the group.

But Gene has her own thoughts about achieving success in the field. "Investigative reporters—and I know some—are not all the same breed," she says, trying to define what others have hesitated to do. The energetic newswoman has been around long enough to see the craft mature. Yet she doesn't believe that Watergate was the end of an era, as some have suggested, or proved that only young reporters like Woodstein can dig out in-depth pieces of national consequence. "I don't intentionally bypass my age (forty-six)—I don't act it. I don't believe I look it either. And I intend to keep at this even from a motorized wheelchair!"

The investigative reporter, she insists, can be a rugged individualist, gregarious or scholarly, "but hopefully we all have a sense of responsibility that makes us constantly aware that we have, through our jobs, the ability to irreparably damage people and institutions—to make or break lives, in other words. And hopefully we all spend a few sleepless nights worrying about our objectivity, our fairness, and our accuracy. I know I do."

There are nights, however, when she can get to sleep satisfied that the long hours, pressures and occasional emotional fatigue are worth it. There are accomplishments other than uncovering corruption, she believes. Such was the case of Jimmy Foster, an ex-runner for some of Milwaukee's best-known bookies. Back in the 1960s, Gene met Jimmy, a cabbie who frequented an eastside tavern, while working on a story about gambling in Milwaukee. Jimmy handled some of her bets at the tracks. That's the account Gene gave the Circuit Court months later when she was on the witness stand describing her experiences to a jury investigating gambling charges. The cabbie-bookie was convicted and fined $250. In her story days later, Gene also criticized an off-duty detective she had observed in the tavern who had "cleaned" a young man of his leather jacket and money in a pool game.

But that's only part of the story. Seven years later,

Gene got a call from the pool-playing detective with a strange request. "Gene, come over to my house—I've got the biggest story you've ever covered," he said. She'd heard the line before but her reporter's instincts said go. *Sentinel* reporter Gerry Hinkley, who wrote about it, picks up the story at that point:

"With some misgivings but with her reporter's curiosity whetted, Gene drove to the detective's house.... Gene was told how Jimmy and Bonnie (his girl friend for years) were living together and that they had a beautiful daughter. For months Joe (the tavern owner) and Dorsey (the detective) had pleaded, 'Jimmy, you love Bonnie. Why don't you marry her?' but he continued to balk.

"However, the night before at Joe's Tavern, Jimmy had issued an ultimatum: 'I'll get married the day Gene Cunningham walks in here and buys me a drink.' 'So will you do it?' Dorsey and Joe asked.

"Within an hour, the three were at Joe's tavern and Jimmy was called over from his flat next door. The cab driver chatted easily with his two friends, failing to recognize the back of the woman seated between them.

"Hey, Jimmy, have a drink on me," said Gene, swinging around on the bar stool with a drink in hand. Jimmy accepted in open-mouthed disbelief.

"The bar was filled with regulars who knew what was happening. Jimmy had to keep his promise. With the double brandy and water still untouched, Jimmy returned to his flat and proposed to Bonnie with Dorsey and his wife, Elsie, as witnesses...."

Her most satisfying investigation?

"That's tough. I've felt very good about several. But I suppose a series on our county board chairman which led to his ultimate conviction for corrupt practices was the most rewarding. It brought about the calling of a special grand jury, his indictment, and his conviction on charges detailed in the investigative series in the *Senti-*

nel months earlier. To me, it's always rewarding to get a crook out of public office, and this is the top office in a heavily populated county that sops up enough tax dollars as it is. The chairman, by the way, was removed from office by state law requiring such action upon conviction for a felony. Eight felony charges were brought against him; all of them dug up and made public in the *Sentinel's* investigative series."

The investigation showed Gene how far the accused will go to protect his turf, too. "The guy even hired a private detective to follow me trying to get something on me to blackmail me out of continuing the investigation and writing the series. Didn't find anything and his efforts just didn't work. I later interviewed the private detective. He was embarrassed. He'd always been a kind of offbeat source for me.

"But you can't let it bother you . . . telling the public something it should know—it must know—and otherwise wouldn't, is important to me. We concentrate heavily on crime, official and governmental corruption, bureaucratic waste and bungling—the very things that cost tax dollars, bilk the public, and make a farce of the ballot box and our entire system of government. To catch and penalize those who illegally profit at public expense—or who bungle their way to high-paying, tax-financed jobs—is satisfying enough for me. Someone has to do it. Law enforcement isn't . . . for a variety of reasons. The press is the only watchdog left and this (investigative reporting) has become a function of the press. I believe properly so."

The belief, in fact, has been entrenched since she graduated from Galesburg High School in the historic west central Illinois community. It was at Knox College in Galesburg that Lincoln debated Stephen Douglas. And it was Galesburg that produced Carl Sandburg, biographer of Lincoln, poet, and editorial writer.

Like many other small town graduates in the state,

Gene went to the University of Illinois. Unlike many, however, she chose a career in journalism. With a degree in her suitcase, Gene found her first job on a small magazine more than a thousand miles away in Aberdeen, South Dakota. That lasted a year and gave her just enough experience to make her next move; the purchase and management of a chain of newspapers and a printing plant in central Illinois. "After eight years there, I went to the Rockford, Illinois, *Register-Republic* as a general assignment reporter, working later into investigative reporting on a Rockford-size scale. I did a brief stint as the Rockford public schools' first public relations director prior to taking a job with the Milwaukee *Sentinel*," she adds.

Although she readily admits that goals and attitudes toward one's work change with age and interests, she believes her role and interest have already passed crucial tests of self-examination. "I don't think *most* people in journalism want to become editors for one thing. If they do, I'm certainly not one of them. As for prestige and power in this field, I think the reporter handling the story has more of that than any editor with a copy pencil. Prestige? How many people even know the name of the editor of their local paper? But they do recognize frequently the name of the bylined reporter. Prestige for editors may come in newspaper circles. Maybe. And money is not going to motivate me to leave reporting. The salary is good and although my editor makes more, he may get bored. I don't."

Management has been more than satisfied with her efforts, let alone her achievements. Gene has won awards from Sigma Delta Chi, the Scripps-Howard Foundation, the National Center for Journalism. the National Federation of Press Women, the Illinois State Press Association, the National Association of Retarded Children, the Milwaukee Press Club, and the Medical Society of Milwaukee County among others. In 1972, she was named "Wisconsin Newsman of the Year" by Sigma Delta Chi ("*Newsman* was what they called it then before they figured out it might be won by a woman. Now they've renamed it *Journalist of the Year*," she points out wryly).

Equally important to her are the contributions she's made to the local, state, and national awards won by the *Sentinel* for investigative reporting series every year since 1972. Each assignment is like a shot of adrenalin, her colleagues say.

A typical day? It starts late and ends late.

"I follow a general kind of pattern, the faces and stories may change but the hours are rather consistent. Take this recent day, for example. I arrived at work mid-morning. I spent maybe an hour or so reading messages left for me and going through my mail and returning telephone calls. I then drove to the south side of the city to interview a pharmacist in connection with a series I'm working on involving kickbacks by pharmacists to nursing homes for drugs sold to Title 19 patients. The interview went well for me—it took until well after the noon hour.

"Got back to the office and had lunch with a bunch of newspaper people in the company cafeteria. I made a telephone call and set up an appointment for dinner with a law enforcement source to discuss an underworld development in Milwaukee that could soon open up trouble. Typed notes from my earlier interviews with pharmacists and nursing home people. At the same time I handled maybe a half dozen phone calls. I had brief chats with reporters and the city editor in the newsroom. I met my law enforcement friend for dinner. Afterward I went with him to his office to go over some of the material he had gathered. I called it quits about 10:30 P.M. To some, it may sound uneventful but the information I gathered alone made it a productive day."

Since Gene is single and without family, her lifestyle revolves around her work and friends. "I have my own home in which another female *Sentinel* reporter and a former domestic employee of my family (now kind of part of the family) live with me. We have a swimming pool and I swim almost daily in the summer to get the kinks and frustrations out. I also have a place in the northern Wisconsin woods (way out where there are no telephones) where I go to hide on weekends and vacations. It's something you've got to have in this work or other kinds of jobs where there is a great deal of concentration, I believe. In the absence of a family, my friends play an important part in my life—as they would even with a family!

"I'm certainly no loner. I'm gregarious as heck. And I can't understand how a loner, in fact, could make it as an investigative reporter. I think it takes an out-going type of person that people are willing to talk to, feel they can trust—someone with a friendly instead of stand-offish approach. I have a lot of friends who began as news sources and now are both. And I have a lot of friends who are on the newspaper staff, too. We socialize together, have poker-playing round-robins and get together quite often, in fact. Loner? No way! I'm the friendly type—at least I think so."

But she doesn't substitute friendliness for guts when it comes to getting hard information from sensitive sources about a sensitive subject.

"I have enough subpoenaes to paper my walls and I stayed out of jail in one case only by virtue of some talented legal work by the paper's attorneys. A stay order came by telephone just as I was beginning an appearance in an adverse examination in connection with the county board chairman case."

What should be done to aid the investigative reporter today?

"I think there should be a shield law but I think there should be cooperation, when possible, between investigative reporters and law enforcement. No way will I go to jail to protect a source who may be a criminal, a corrupt official or some other clod who should be in jail himself! The question, of course, is what kind of shield law should we have. And I don't really know."

Gene is also convinced the newspaper must permit the investigative reporter to spend all of his/her time on such special stories. "Certainly they should. Who else is going to expose and catch up with the corruption and bungling, the crime and tax waste? And there's plenty to go around. Law enforcement is not doing it. It's up to us. As for involving the investigative reporter in other duties, I don't think they can double up and be effective either place. I am full-time investigative—and it works well that way. If I have to go cover a governmental meeting or do an interview unrelated to investigative reporting immediately the thought of those involved is that they're being investigated or the *Sentinel* thinks something is wrong—it just doesn't work. At the same time, I feel I have to be free to follow my nose in order to get the job done. Lots of hours and days are totally unproductive but then something clicks and the whole picture starts fitting together piece by piece. You have to have the talk time, the thought time, the time to plan, plot and plod till it all starts coming together. I have it here on this paper—totally."

The argument that distresses her most is from those who believe the investigative reporter must observe certain responsibilities. Such criticism has been traditional among those who support secrecy to protect national interests where illegal acts and wrongdoings have taken place.

"Responsibilities such as national security, hazards, or threats to innocent victims sound far too dramatic," she retorts. "I once knew an investigative reporter who said he wouldn't get married because of the danger, the hazard involved in his life due to the nature of the work. May have sounded good to his girl friend but it's sheer melodrama 99 percent of the time! As for responsibility for others and their protection, if you're not willing to accept that, you're in the wrong business! You *are* your sources and the trust and faith they have in you. Without them—unless you protect them and respect their confidences—you might as well plan on covering the Ladies' Aid or the Boy Scout Jamboree because that's where you'll end up. That's as sacred to the reporter as the relationship between lawyer and client. Without sources, you'll not make an investigative reporter. Once you fink or endanger a cooperative source, the news travels—especially if you're working in crime or governmental areas and you might as well forget it. Your first success became your last investigative story."

Photo of Ted Driscoll by Arman Hatsian of the Hartford *Courant*.

8

Ted Driscoll:
"You Need Perspective When You Have to Hurt People"

Unlike the famous of the reporting world—Anderson, Bernstein, and Woodward—about the only people who recognize Ted Driscoll's byline in the Hartford *Courant* are his boss, those he investigates, and his wife.

Answers one and three really count, of course. He wants his boss—the managing editor—to know he's on the job. His wife? Well, since she's another *Courant* reporter, it's a matter of family pride.

Theodore A. Driscoll is *the* investigative reporter on the Hartford, Connecticut *Courant*. Hartford is the capital of the state and the hub of the insurance industry in the East if not the country. His job is a coveted position held by a mere few hundred on a small portion of the nation's more than 1,750 dailies. He's paid his dues, too—ten years as a reporter for the *Courant*—yet he's had little recognition for the abrasive kinds of stories he's done. "A continuing problem for me is keeping perspective on the people who get hurt by my stories," he laments. "Often I start feeling sorry for them before the article is written. Then I have to step back and get perspective. My responsibility is to the public, not to the thief I'm writing about. I find that most corrupt people, incidentally, are very likable."

Ted didn't get his principles of the press in a journalism school or on a list of prestigious papers. He took some courses while finishing his bachelor's in English at the University of Connecticut. He started at Colby and then transferred to the state university at Storrs. For two years after graduation, he sampled life, lifestyles, and all kinds of jobs. "I was a social worker in Los Angeles, a cab driver, Fuller Brush man, a mason's laborer, landscaper, truck driver, ski bum, bartender, factory worker, nightclub and ski lodge manager. But I hadn't worked on a paper until I applied at the *Courant*," he recalls.

He's not sure they've all helped his work but he knows that being a generalist—knowing something about a number of things—can be useful to a newspaperman.

It took the intuition of a bartender and the logic and savvy of a city cab driver, for example, to piece together the fact that a transportation commissioner had omittted from a state report a conclusion that major highway construction was needed to handle traffic at the site of the state's first racetrack. It was the kind of story where you had to have sources, a solid understanding of the chronology of events, and a keen recall to reconstruct the meetings and dialogue that had taken place with those in charge. Then too it was the kind of story where you had to know the motives of those for and against portions of the project and their reasons.

"It was no Watergate, certainly, yet it was one of those investigative pieces that got behind official pronouncements and attempted to keep government and political officialdom aware that they can't avoid what they don't want at their own discretion," another *Courant* reporter explained.

Ted's story in February 1975 on the highway construction project included excerpts from documents that demonstrated how the editing was done and why. It was accompanied by a sidebar story explaining the commissioner's reasons. In the hands of a regular reporter unfamiliar with the labyrinth of details and background information it might have been an unintelligible story to the average Hartfordite.

"I like learning how things really work," Ted says. "Unraveling a complex, corrupt scheme, fashioned by people sure they would not get caught, is great fun. It is also interesting to learn about people who run things in our society. Some are decent, others shrewdly corrupt, and some are talentless and not very smart but willing to do things decent people wouldn't do.

"I like catching people who think they can screw the public with impunity. It is particularly rewarding if they are hypocrites. Part of it is an ego thing, I suppose. It's a nice feeling, like laying out a bully. Beyond that, I really think we would stifle in our own corruption if decent people didn't pull together now and then to keep the greedy in check. I like the mechanics of investigative reporting, getting the information and then putting together all the tidbits. I also like the challenge of taking on big and powerful people. And I think it's something that needs doing, so I feel good about my work."

Several stories Ted feels especially good about attacked the administration of former Governor Thomas J. Meskill. The *Courant* discovered in the spring of 1973 that jobs and promotions within the state civil service were being used as rewards in a scheme of illegal changes of party affiliations to increase Republican enrollments.

In a copyrighted *Courant* front-page story, Driscoll said, "The scheme affects several state departments and is coordinated at Republican State Headquarters. Many interviews for state jobs are held at GOP headquarters and job seekers are referred to state agencies after they agree to solicit registrations and do other work for the party. Some applicants fill out a form which reads at the top: 'Confidential for Governor Thomas J. Meskill.' . . . There is no evidence that the forms are seen by the governor.

"These workers and others already in state service and seeking advancement, solicit people to sign applications for changing party registrations from Democrat or unaffiliated to Republican.

"Many changeover applications are illegal because the applicant did not personally appear before the justice of the peace. False notarization is a felony in Connecticut. . . . Hundreds of illegal registrations have been located on file with registrars of voters throughout the state. . . . Some of the people soliciting these changeover registrations for the justices of the peace are in jobs funded by the federal Emergency Employment Act (EEA). Federal law prohibits the hiring of EEA employees for political reasons and restricts the political activities of those hired. Others soliciting changeover applications are in the state's civil service which also restricts political activity."

The story was one of a number he did that were particularly difficult because of the popularity of the governor. "Meskill was a likable man, even I liked him," Ted insists. "And it took a lot of doing to make people realize that he and his administration were involved in such activities. Several articles let the public see that side of him."

Aware that he didn't have the clout of an Anderson, Bernstein, or Woodward, Ted compensated by digging deeper than anyone else into the governor's operations and the activities of the state's public works commissioner. Months of careful research produced a major exposé linking the governor, the public works commissioner, and a New Britain realtor in the purchase of a building for the Greater Hartford Community College. It was Driscoll's investigative efforts that revealed the two government officials were shareholders along with the realtor in a commercial venture in the city.

"The secret business relationship raises the possibility of a conflict of interest because Meskill and (the public works commissioner), as state officials, influence decisions to purchase or lease buildings in which (the realtor) as a broker may have an interest," Driscoll and reporter Stan Simon said in a copyrighted page-one piece.

The *Courant* team discovered that the realtor had brought together two developers who arranged to buy the building for use by the state college while the state officials ignored the same opportunity. "Two days after the developers obtained an option to buy the building, the state for the first time publicly advertised it needed college space."

Though the governor and the public works director denied that there was conflict of interest (and both were given opportunities in the same edition that carried the story explaining the secret arrangement), the *Courant* investigators raised serious doubts. The story was one of a series Driscoll had uncovered on state leasing practices. "The series was very satisfying, I think, because the state commissioner on public works all but called me a liar in attempting to defend himself against my first article, then was thoroughly discredited by my follow-up articles. He had always succeeded in maneuvering his way out of things. It didn't work with me," Ted recalls.

The satisfaction of doing such stories, he adds, makes up for the long hours, the painstaking research frequently needed to support such articles, and the threats and pressure that surround virtually every major investigative task. But he doesn't see the accomplishments as rungs on the ladder to promotion to more administrative tasks at the newspaper—at least not yet. "Being an editor strikes me as being dull. Perhaps it won't one day, if I tire of chasing stories. I like helping other reporters and sometimes like telling other people what to do, so perhaps one day.... It's more likely, though, that I'll attempt a book."

Having a wife as a colleague at work and a partner at home has its benefits and frustrations, Ted admits. "My wife covers the state capitol at the *Courant*, which is rather sensitive, considering some of the stories I've done about state officials. Long ago, though, we made a house rule that my work was not to be discussed. The intrigue occasionally upsets her. Sometimes I have to meet people at odd hours and sometimes I get calls at home. But I try with fair success to compartmentalize my work. Even though I have an office at home and I occasionally work there rather than at the paper, I try not to mix work with any of my other activities. I also try to keep reasonable hours whenever possible. But when I'm about to go into print with a big story or things start breaking all around me, I forget compartmentalization and just work, sometimes around the clock. But I try to do this only when necessary."

Ted sees himself as a loner primarily who on occasion "goes public. I work alone on most things and I also enjoy doing many things by myself although sometimes I'm gregarious. I like to watch people. For instance, I really enjoy walking for hours in a city just watching people. This is particularly pleasant in a foreign city."

What's a day like for an investigative reporter on a paper outside a major metropolitan area such as Boston, New York, or Washington?

There are differences, of course, but the similarities are noticeable too.

"I'm up at 8:00 A.M. usually, shower and read the

Courant while eating a light breakfast. At the office at nine on a recent morning, I glanced through material from the Securities Exchange Commission on two corporations. Typed out notes on a seven-hour interview I had with a lawyer in Boston the previous day," he recounts, ticking off the way his day begins. "I keep daysheets separating notes into the major projects I am working on. This particular day I typed out three daysheets covering two interviews and several phone calls. I got a phone call from someone with information on a series I did more than a year ago. Several other phone calls during the day—most of them pertaining to projects I have not really gotten into yet. I keep in touch with these sources so they will know of my continuing interest.

"For lunch I ate a sandwich at my desk, my usual routine unless I take someone to lunch for an interview. I spoke with another reporter who has come to me for advice on a project she is doing. My boss called me into his office to hear another reporter describe some peculiar goings-on on his beat. They relate to a project I am doing but we do not tell that to the reporter. Instead, I just pick his brain and advise him on how to get further information. During the day, I glance through competing area newspapers, and the New York *Times.* Before leaving the office, I type up a daysheet for this day and jot down some things I want to do the next day. I leave about 7:00 P.M. My wife and I have a late dinner. I read for a short while and get to bed about midnight."

Sources, Ted emphasizes, must be protected but "there should be no shield laws to be tampered with by some future Nixon. What the law gives, the law can take away. Reporters, I believe, are better off relying on the First Amendment. Newspapers should get into investigative reporting rather cautiously. Unless done with integrity and intelligence, investigative reporting can do more harm than good."

How does an investigative reporter see danger in the popularity and growth of the field?

"A newspaper should develop a staff of good daily reporters and try the best among them as investigative reporters. If the investigative reporter does not produce, he should simply be reassigned. He should not be pressured into a story. An investigative reporter in need of a story can be a very dangerous fellow. The investigative reporter should be mindful of the truth rather than of libel when he decides how far to go with a story. His concern must be in telling the truth rather than getting a headline."

While each investigative reporter has to use a variety of techniques and rely upon successful experiences to elicit information, Ted is concerned about the means justifying the ends in such work. "Many investigative reporters use deceit and tricks to get what they want. I try not to, although I don't always identify myself as a reporter and I suppose some one could rap me for it. Sometimes I employ a harmless deception. My rule, though, is not to do anything unethical or illegal and to do nothing that would embarrass me or my paper if I got caught at it. Like all good reporters, I'm very protective of confidential sources and I'm willing to go to jail if I have to, to protect them."

His sources risk losing their jobs or going to jail in some instances depending upon the sensitivity of the material, he says. For example, it was through his sources in 1973 that he was able to uncover a story about political patronage that bordered on violations of the law.

"Hundreds of persons have joined state service without taking competitive examinations. In some cases, they replaced classified career employes who were forced to retire, transferred to deadend jobs or laid off. . . . The *Courant* has evidence of widespread instances of favoritism in the hiring and promotion of state employes. . . .

Those favored by the abuses are often active in Republican politics."

Such claims have to be supported by solid research, Ted maintains, or you're in serious trouble. It's not too difficult to find disgruntled workers who have been dismissed or mistreated when political administrations change hands. However, the real task is supporting charges of actual violations of the law by talking to sources on both sides of the issue to verify the complaints and then secure documentation to turn circumstantial evidence or hearsay into fact. "When you write that the *'Courant* has evidence of widespread instances . . . ,' it must mean just that," he says.

The stories come and go and, like so many others in such a specialty, Ted's concern is sustaining himself. Investigative reporting fatigues, experienced news people say, because a big piece can make others appear anticlimactic.

Where does Ted Driscoll see himself in ten years?

"Ten years is a long time in the life of a reporter. It is likely, though, I will be doing this kind of work or something related to it. I might do more in-depth digging and be writing a book ten years from now.

"But I know what I don't want to be doing: working nine to five at the same thing every day and worrying about my retirement."

Photo of Nick Gage courtesy of the New York *Times*.

9

Nick Gage:
"The Loneliness Can
Get to You"

Investigative reporters are outgoing people who lead exciting lives and are respected by their colleagues.

Right?

Wrong. At least New York *Times* investigative reporter and resident Mafia expert Nick Gage doesn't think so.

"Most people don't really know how lonely this work can be. You're generally not liked by your colleagues, or let's say you feel you aren't. Part of it, I suppose, is the arrangements you have and part of it is that you get more space—more attention. If somebody covering hospitals has to do a story every day, for example, and you only do one every so often, there's a difference, see. Of course he probably wouldn't want to do the digging you do. Part of it basically is that most reporters like camaraderie—you know, to go to the bar across the street and trade stuff and talk shop. Which can lead to discussions you don't want to be in if you're an investigative reporter because of the sensitive things involved in your work. You just can't take those chances. Most investigative reporters are skeptical of everybody, including other reporters, so there's a feeling of mistrust, too. When you work on a story a couple of months you really get so involved you don't care about anybody else either."

His comment is like a self-portrait. Nick Gage sees investigative reporting as a personal thing; his lifestyle and work hours are shaped to meet the needs of sources and stories. A tough way to live; but it's been successful for him.

It was Nick Gage who told readers about the inner workings of the Mafia, its soldiers, lieutenants, and dons during the 1960s. The stories led to several books. The research has surfaced from time to time as the foundation for other stories. In December 1974, it was Nick's sources and background that produced the New York *Times* article questioning the authenticity of the as-told-to autobiography of the late "Lucky" Luciano, a book that grossed more than a million dollars before it was published.

Investigative reporting can be a pressure cooker, too, as publishers seek more blockbusting stories, and law enforcement agencies scrutinize the reporter's contacts. But Nick has a reputation for protecting sources at the risk of his own job. "I don't like to go on fishing expeditions. What really eats at me is if I've been unfair to someone. That keeps me up nights. No story is worth seeing someone killed either. After Joe Gallo was killed, one of the gunmen talked in Los Angeles and I found out about it. The police told me, 'Don't use it because we haven't found the man's wife and family,' and I didn't because she would have been killed."

Like the undercover cop, Nick plays roles, too. "You have to be a little of a con man—you have to bluff your way sometimes to get information," he says. But there are boundaries. The New York *Times* does not permit him to go undercover to gather information nor does it allow him to pay for information. The *Times* expects him to rely on his myriad of sources ("I've got several close sources and maybe several hundred all over the world"), his patience, and his newsman's intuition to pull information together for his stories. And it works.

He used his sources and seven weeks of patient research to dig into a story about a $4 million swindle from the Penn Central Railroad. Two Washington lawyers were subsequently indicted. It was one of his most satisfying stories, he says.

"The swindle was set up through a variety of dummy corporations and Liechtenstein trusts and the whole schmear. It's the kind of investigative reporting that isn't done much. To do that kind of investigative reporting and make it understandable to the ordinary newspaper reader is difficult, and to get documentation to prove your case is difficult, too. The particular thing about this investigation is that a House-Senate Committee looked into the disappearance of the money, and they blamed it on a German financier who had transferred the money through a Liechtenstein company. Then I found a record showing that there was a Panamanian company used in the transfer that really belonged to two lawyers, not the financier. The committee has something like nine investigators and they missed one little document which I found in the Securities and Exchange Commission files going back to 1958. It illustrates the kind of digging you have to do for those stories and why I suppose so few are done."

But he doesn't always have a document in hand. And that's where sources play a vital role. For example, the story he broke during the Nixon presidency concerning the ITT investigation came on a chance meeting with a source.

"I was in Washington on another story, and I was going to take the plane back to New York. I had about forty minutes, so I went to see a guy who has been a source of mine just to say hello and to touch base with him. I like to maintain visual contact with my sources... nothing special. He happened to have access to the tape— the conversation between Nixon and Richard Kleindienst, the attorney general. I quoted the tape right there in which the president called Kleindienst and swore at him and told him to lay off the case. I got the story in one afternoon just by staying in touch with a source. I like that story, too, because there were loads of stories and rumors about Nixon at that time. I was able to work with direct conversation ... something that was quite clear. It wasn't speculation. That's hard to do, and when I'm able to get that kind of verification, it's like a document."

On other stories, he's had to start from scratch. A series he likes to recall took him to South America. It was about heroin and cocaine traffic. "I spent eight weeks in Latin America and I went in cold. But I got names of people being paid off, government officials and so on, and I was able to get very damaging information. Rather than say a general did this or a minister did that, I said General So and So and Minister So and So in print. On a story like that I make sure that whenever I run into somebody I make a note of it on paper or in my head. I wait until enough sources pile up in a particular area and I've got a starting point. If you see your sources don't have the information you need, it then becomes a matter of winning the trust of others you meet quickly. This is the key thing in those kinds of stories. I worked alone on the drug series and I had to gain confidences fast.

"That's the trick really. It's very hard to learn and it's very hard to fake. The only way you can do it is through empathy. You have to like the person you're dealing with and he or she has to like you. If that empathy doesn't exist, you can't establish ground on which to work. Why? Because it can get very expensive. For a story on drugs in Europe, *Newsday* used up to twelve men over a period of a year and spent close to $300,000, I'm told. As a result of that kind of experience, *Newsday* broke up its investigative team, although they won the Pulitzer Prize for it."

Nick rarely uses his office or the telephone to gather sensitive material. "What works, though, is seeing people face to face. It's just a different thing. For example, we called Hugh Sloan (a key figure in the Bernstein and Woodward Watergate stories) several different times—the *Times* did—and he wouldn't talk to us on the phone about Watergate. Woodward and Bernstein went to see Hugh Sloan and he was their main source—they got there first. That's one case that illustrates the limitations of the phone. Occasionally I get information on the phone. Very rarely though will someone give me sensitive information over the telephone. I use it to make appointments to see somebody face to face."

Working with sources in the newsroom is virtually impossible, he insists. "I deal with Arthur Gelb, the metropolitan editor, even when I'm overseas. The only exception is when I'm in Washington and then I run my material through the bureau there. I basically like to find somebody to have contact with and the meetings can be almost anywhere. Then I take the responsibilities in dealing with them. Management goes to extremes sometimes in trying to handle you or keep tabs on you. Either they've got a guy who works a lot of chicken shit and is in the paper every other day with garbage or they leave you alone. Then when you don't produce anything in six months they say 'Gee, what a waste.' So they drop investigative reporting because they're not getting anything from you. Basically, I think management has got to say 'Look, you're on your own. If we hear something we'll tell you. In order for us to justify someone, though, we'll need six pieces a year. . . .' "

Yet he doesn't believe the newspaper owes it to the investigative reporter to make special arrangements beyond the freedom of his work schedule. "I think the investigative reporter has to be the most carefully chosen person any editor hires," he contends. "Almost every story an investigative reporter does is going to hurt somebody. You've got to be very sure that you have a very strong person in the spot."

There's little regularity to Nick's day at work or his hours. "It depends at what point of development I am in the story," he says. "I come in about 11 o'clock in the morning. I usually go through to see what calls I've had and make return calls. Then I'll meet a source for lunch and I'll do some kind of legwork in the afternoon . . . going to SEC offices, county clerk's office, DA's office, something like that. I get back about 5:30 and see what mail I've got and I go home at 7:00. But that's deceiving. Those are the regular hours, you could say. When I'm working on something I will probably start at 8:00 in the morning—I'll get up around 7:00—and I will usually meet somebody for breakfast—a federal law enforcement officer usually because they start to work about 8:30 and it's hard to see them at the office. I may have a hundred breakfasts with somebody to develop him as a source. Well, not every day but at least two or three times a week. It's not really for a story then. When the time comes, I go to the person, face to face, and say, 'Look, you gotta tell me.' I usually can get it.

"There are some days, for example, once every three or four weeks that are my Brooklyn days. I'll go out to Brooklyn and stop by all the sources I've got out there. . . . You know, merchants and so on, just to get to talk with them. Sometimes, they'll give me a bit of information that will make a story. . . . Sometimes they'll run into something two days after I've seen them, and they'll say 'Gee, I've got to call Nick.' Whereas if I hadn't touched base with them they might not think it was important."

But he doesn't always trust the source's intentions either. 'Sometimes they will deliberately give me a wrong detail. Perhaps for their own protection, they believe. For instance, I wrote a piece on Mario Biaggi (10th Dist. congressman from New York who became entangled in a campaign issue regarding testimony given a grand jury and subsequent information he gave to the public). I said he had taken the Fifth Amendment thirty times. Actually it was sixteen. Did my source give me wrong information to divert suspicion from himself? Maybe. But the story was substantially correct. A source may say, 'We've got a really big one coming up but I can't discuss it.' And I'll say, 'Who else might know about it?' If I get a piece I can bluff the rest of the way."

It was Gage's bluff, for instance, that brought answers concerning the tale of deception and intrigue involving the New York Metropolitan Museum's million dollar Euphronios vase. His investigation began with one scrap of information: the vase's date of entry into the United States, August 31, 1972. A contact at the U.S. Customs Office at John F. Kennedy International Airport demonstrated his loyalty by searching 16,000 entries to find the correct data for Nick. On a gamble, he took his fragment of the story and flew to Europe where he talked to several more sources. Then he jetted to Rome where he made a dinner date with the man who delivered the vase to the Met. As they dined, Gage dropped bits and pieces of what he knew with the nonchalance of an old poker pro. His dinner guest nervously filled in the details of what he knew of a tale of chicanery that led from Rome to Zurich to Lebanon.

But a bluff can be dangerous and Gage is well aware of the consequences. New York *Times* executives were nervous about his story on Biaggi. A number of *Times*-men had come up with nothing after tracking down the same lead. What made Gage so sure, when the congressman had gone on three television stations to protest his innocence? "I was absolutely sure . . . I trusted my source," he retorted. The pressure continued to mount after Gage's article was published. United States Attorney (at the time) Whitney North Seymour, Jr., threatened to have the reporter appear before the grand jury and reveal his source or be cited for contempt. "You just decide you're not going to reveal sources," he said. "I broke no law in getting the story and that's about all I was going to say if they called."

Does the pressure and the nearly twenty-four-hour involvement in his work every day interfere with family life?

"Sure it does. It can be difficult. I've got two small children and my wife who incidentally is a graduate of the Columbia School of Journalism and who's a journalist, too. She's helped a lot. She understands what I've got to do. I'm not a talkative person. I don't like to talk about what I'm working on in my head . . . it's a pain. My wife understands that, though she may listen in on the phone sometimes to find out what I'm doing. She helps me keep track of people who call me and she also helps when I write out my really long articles. It's very nice to have another ear, you know."

In Nick's opinion a good family life can really help an investigative reporter. "You've got to be persistent and have a strong identity, but most investigative reporters I know also happen to have good home lives, too. You can't be going through four divorces and do an effective job in this field. It's not the gay bachelor type who makes it but somebody who has good strong roots.

I think that gives you a basic sense of strength and imagination day to day."

Unlike other areas of media where the need to compete is strong, investigative reporters have a closer, more fraternal bond, Nick suggests. "Most of the investigative reporters I know are not necessarily involved in competition. In fact, most are friends with each other. They really don't compete. If my editor says go after that story and I know a good friend of mine is on it, I'll say, 'Sorry, I've been ordered to do it,' and, you know, I'll give it my all. Generally, if I hear a good friend is investigating a particular story I won't go after it because these stories are very hard to get. Once somebody's started on one it's very hard to catch up. Look at Watergate for example. Most editors want you to go after it, of course. But I don't like to do stories that are somebody else's or where I'm trying to catch up. You do a shallow job and it really shows. An editor, though, has a different obligation.

"I'm really a reporter. . . . I consider myself a reporter. But I like to take pride in the way I present my stories. I like to think my stories are better written than most newspaper stories. I work at that. If you read my stories, I think they're better structured and I work at that, too. Some reporters I know don't work at that . . . they don't care that much about it . . . I do."

Persistence, he maintains, has been his success. "If I think something is there, I stick to it until I get it. But at the same time, I'm willing to wash out a story. That is one of the major problems of investigative reporters today, I think. If they feel they have devoted a week or two or more to a story, they've got to come out with a story. You see a lot of stories that don't say anything. The pressure is on to do a story—any story. For example, during the last election, I was investigating one of the political candidates. I spent five weeks on it and I had enough hearsay material to make a story. It would have been front page but it was simply hearsay and I went to my editor and said, 'I'm not going to do that story, you know . . . it's simply not hard enough to go on.' So I think another strength of mine is knowing when to quit as well as not giving up. If I suffer a setback I get a double rush of adrenalin or something and it pushes me to work even harder. Also I have a realistic sense that enables me to judge what is the little story and when to go after the one with substance. When it's not there, I pull out."

That realistic sense has been a factor in Nicholas Gatzoyiannis' life since he came to America from Greece when he was nine and later took the Americanized byline, Nick Gage. At fourteen, he proved himself equal to the kids on the block in Worcester, Massachusetts, when he won a $1,000 essay—in English, no less. He attended nearby Boston University and was editor of the student newspaper his sophomore year. Before he left, he got his first taste of newspaper work with the Associated Press. It was the Boston *Herald Traveler,* however, where he tried investigative work. At twenty-seven, he wrote his first exposé when he got a job inside a school for the retarded as an attendant and wrote about the conditions. He later worked for the *Wall Street Journal* before joining the *Times.*

If there's a weakness in the Gage game plan, it's after a story is finished.

"I just don't like to follow up on the story. I don't like the everyday kind of thing trying to come up with something new. I feel my job is to do my story—to lay out what it is. I think the people who have the responsibility to take action on it should do the rest. I don't feel it's my job to call them up and say, 'What are you going to do about it now?' I just don't like to create my own news— I'm not an advocate. It's not my nature."

He's had some regrets about stories he's done, too.

"I've finished stories on the Jewish mob and Jews have gotten angry and I've done stories on the Italian mob and the Italians have gotten mad. Yes, it bothers me. Anybody can pick up the phone and call me. I have nobody to fend off the phone calls. It's hard for me to hang up on a guy. There are tough things about this job. One is the abusive calls you get and the other, the kooks you run into without trying. People are always coming up to you with information about anything . . . you know, tremendous conspiracies out to get them. They all say, 'This is bigger than Watergate,' and it's actually some trouble they're having with their wives, or their estranged spouse, or some judge who ruled against them in a civil case and it becomes an obsession with them. They develop miles and miles of material and they all want you to listen. You can never send any of them away without talking to them because they just may have something or know something that's important. . . . You waste a lot of time to be sure, but there's always the chance, you know. Of course, there are a few you turn away because of the general drift or lack of it in what they're saying . . . it's a real pain."

Some journalists and journalism educators believe investigative reporting has merely become a fad—a pseudoscience—blown out of proportion. Nick agrees it has been exaggerated by stories such as Watergate. But he also believes it has demonstrated its importance. A few reporters, in fact, have given it a new status because of their skills, he contends.

"There are a few who have made a career of developing sources; developing accesses other reporters can and have used. It's been a lifetime job for them, not a fad. I would say that perhaps a half dozen of that kind of person—reporters like Jack Anderson, Jack Nelson, Jerry Landeau, Stanley Penn—work on sources all the time.

Carl Bernstein doesn't really do the kind of investigative story that I'm talking about. If Woodward and Bernstein had come up to New York at the time of Watergate they wouldn't have come up with anything. In fact, I don't think they see themselves spending the rest of their lives doing that kind of work. I think such a view of the field is true of them. But there are other reporters it's just not true about."

It's certainly not true about Nick Gage.

Photo of James A. Haught courtesy of James A. Haught.

10

Sending People to Jail Doesn't Give Jim Haught Any Pleasure

Jim Haught lives in what the rest of the country commonly refers to as a "chronically depressed area." West Virginia. It's a place where textbooks can arouse people to commit violence; where smog hangs so thick over the northern valleys it makes Los Angeles look like an environmental haven.

It's also a place where corruption in government has been as commonplace as in Chicago and New York. But few like to talk or read about such "local" problems when there is so much sin on the East and West Coasts. And pity the messenger who brings such bad local tidings.

Enter Jim Haught. The investigative reporter of the Charleston *Gazette;* he's been writing about local skeletons for the past six years. In his opinion, the West Virginia capital is where the action is, and probably always has been. When he finally got there at seventeen (he was born and raised in rural West Virginia and was one of thirteen who graduated from a tiny mountain district school), he wanted to stay. He worked as a delivery boy, then as an usher, to pay the tuition to attend local college classes. He got his first break some time later. He was offered steady work as an apprentice printer in the Charleston *Daily Mail* composing room. His secret desire? To be a reporter.

Although he had no background for the work to speak of and there was plenty of competition for reporting jobs, Jim decided strategy was the answer. He went to the city editor and offered to work at no pay in the newsroom on his days off from typesetting. It was a proposal few hard-nosed editors could turn down. Seven months later, the *Gazette* offered the ambitious beginner a full-time reporting job. He's been with the morning daily ever since, except for a seven-month stint as press aide to a senator, during which he gained thirty pounds and developed his first ulcer. He's covered police, city hall, courts, schools, suburbs, and religion. During a five-year period, he was night and weekend editor on the paper. But it was the offbeat challenges he enjoyed most. Consequently, he was the man editors turned to for such exotic assignments as snake-handling churches, nudist camps, topless nightclubs, John Birch Society meetings, professional gambling, and other bits and pieces of bizarre life. When he wasn't determining the pedigree of a minister's snake, he also reviewed musicals and movies.

In 1970, *Gazette* editors Harry Hoffmann and Dallas Higbee decided the morning paper needed a full-time investigative reporter. Their choice? Jim Haught. They've never regretted the decision and neither has Haught. Others have, though. Jim's stories have brought federal, state, and local authorities to their doors with warrants. Such success has brought enemies, threats, and intimidation along with the pangs of conscience that occur when one sees the anguish on the faces of the innocent victims of such stories, the families of the guilty.

"As for all my corruption work, I have to admit I enjoy some electrifying sense of the risks and the importance of it," he says. You can sense his feeling of accomplishment. "When we're breaking a scandal on the governor or the attorney general, which has ugly criminal implications, there's a tingle of wondering if the impact will bring grand jury investigations, etc., or if the accused will strike back with an expensive lawsuit."

Yet he's well aware of the impact of his stories, too. "What I said about such investigations doesn't give me pleasure, though. I've actually felt bad about seeing some of those involved go to prison and have their wives tell me about their weeping children. My work has caused five felony convictions and a sixth is pending. But this hasn't been pleasurable to me because it has been endless combat, lawsuits, recriminations, and bitterness from injured families," he adds, and the softness of his voice is persuasive evidence. "I guess I'm a little ambivalent at times about this work. I 'feel alive' only when I'm breaking a biggie and I feel restless and frustrated when cases fizzle or I can't get much. Yet when we fend off the libel suits and get a conviction, I usually feel sorry for the guy going to prison."

While he's won several national awards for his investigations, his most satisfying story was an obscure item buried in the musty Kanawha County Courthouse files. He received little recognition for the story, merely a good feeling inside. "It was the most purely rewarding thing I did," he says as he describes the tender love story he found hidden in 1860 handwritten wills and courthouse records. "A white plantation owner had taken one of his slave women as a permanent mate and had eleven children by her. . . . He wrote several wills and other documents to guarantee that she and the children would inherit all his lands. He finally was killed by white neighbors. This story never had been recorded in any West Virginia history books. My article explained for the first time why the largest black community of the state exists near Charleston. It was tantalizing to search through those century-old buried records and find bits of the story, like a detective gathering little pieces of evidence one after another."

But it's the digging that Jim enjoys, especially when he unearths a topic of solid substance. Each story is different, he adds, yet there is a noticeable pattern. "Tips come in by the dozens. When you become known, people phone and write all the time with more allegations than you can check out. Some of it is petty tripe; judge so-and-so has a mistress. Some of it is paranoid distortions by zanies who keep calling and calling. Much of it, however, comes from self-serving sources. One guy, for example, told me about a worker who was embezzling from patients at a state hospital. It turned out to be his wife and he wanted her indicted so he could get custody of the children.

"If a tip seems promising you follow logical avenues. If it's a consumer gripe, I call friendly sources in the city and state consumer protection offices to see if any complaints have been filed and I check the state and federal records for any fraud suits against the company. I look for tax liens or judgments against the firm which can indicate a fly-by-night nearly ready to fly.

"If the tip says some bureaucrat is cheating on expense accounts or shaking down state vendors, I try to get the tipster to lead me to someone who has first-hand evidence, then I try to persuade that person to sign an affidavit even on the condition that his name won't be published. Usually I search the agency's expense vouchers or purchase orders. I'll talk to a chum inside the state investigative agency and tell him what I know, then I watch his reaction. You always watch reactions. It's important to have friends in all the prosecutor's offices, the securities division, the detective bureaus, the IRS intelligence unit, etc. They usually won't tell you anything about grand jury testimony or new cases, especially the IRS agents won't, but they'll sometimes warn you when you have bad info. They can keep you from making serious blunders.

"Working for a morning paper has certain advantages because you can call or visit people in the privacy of their homes at night after they've had a couple of martinis and they're freer to talk. Call a federal agent at his office and you put him in a bind with his chief. You shut him up for good.

"In the greatest tradition of newsmen, I seek to get by with the least amount of work, and I'm inclined to follow the easiest-looking tips; something that can be found tucked away in court records, pinned down with a few phone calls or obtained by writing a Freedom of Information request to a federal office. I keep enormous files on consumer ripoffs, securities swindles, bribery cases, police corruption, election fraud, etc. Sometimes a minor entry on a public record, such as a federal tax lien or a bankruptcy or a court deposition, ties a lot of things together and makes a revelation.

"My publisher doesn't want quickie investigations-by-telephone. He keeps pushing for research into tough things such as the competence of judges or the efficiency of charities. These jobs wear you out because you have to go to many, many records and sources. But they usually produce better original work.

"I'm just talking about the printable cases, though. So much other work winds up nowhere. After messing around with 20 phone calls or trips to the records, you still have nothing tangible enough sometimes. I have bushels of old batches of notes that I keep hanging onto, waiting for something to clinch the information some-day . . ."

Jim's perseverance and penchant for examining and re-examining tales of financial wheeling and dealing and political intrigue set him apart from the reportorial genre. Tracking financial illegalities causes the average newspaper generalist to stick with the obvious; charges and counter-charges made during election-year campaigns and litigations. Real cases of financial scandal, he insists, take months—sometimes years—to document and disclose. The six years he spent investigating the long-running scandal involving a four-state chain of savings and loan offices is a good example.

"In 1971 and 1972, I exposed three consumer frauds involving the company's largest finance office in Charleston. The third disclosure caused a federal probe which resulted in a one-hundred-nine-count fraud indictment against the finance company," Jim explains. "In 1973, I found the company had lavishly entertained the West Virginia banking commissioner on private jet trips while the company was seeking a state bank charter. I also discovered that the company had installed a complete bank, vault and all, without first obtaining a charter."

But he kept the file open because there were unanswered questions and loose ends. Diligent research over familiar terrain—state documents and state sources—continued to provide more questions than answers. "In 1974, I revealed that the state banking commissioner had falsified travel expense accounts. There was an indictment but the case was quashed on a technicality. Later in the same year, the company—Diversified Mountaineer Corporation—went bankrupt and while squads of federal and state investigators entered the picture, I continued to find more material. I discovered, for example, that the DMC president borrowed $300,000 from the company without collateral and he devised bonuses to boost his income to $150,000 a year." The president's girl friend, meanwhile, had bought a mansion and paid off a $75,000 mortgage in four months, the reporter added. The president of DMC pleaded guilty to fraud and became a government witness in 1975.

Such investigative pieces generate pressures of all kinds against the reporter, the newspaper, and the paper's management. Yet, as Davis Taylor, publisher of the award-winning Boston *Globe*, told an American Newspaper Publishers Association audience in 1974 during the zenith of Watergate reporting, newspapers can ask questions of people who make decisions for those who cannot ask for themselves. Full-time investigative units on large and small newspapers provide healthy implications for the profession and the country, he added.

"And it's a trend—so far as newspapers are concerned—that is way overdue. It is something that newspapers can do better than any other medium. Despite inevitable charges that this constitutes initiating the news rather than reacting to it, I must cast my vote for more aggressive investigative reporting. At the same time, we must never lose sight of the need to be scrupulously fair in this kind of effort. Investigative journalism isn't a carte blanche for slipshod, inaccurate, or malicious reporting. On the contrary, it requires more rigorous standards of accuracy, integrity, and fair play than ever. When newspapers become involved in aggressive, investigative journalism, they're dealing with the highest possible stakes. And all the ethics of the profession must be scrupulously observed."

The words have special meaning to Jim. The risks are too great and the public too critical to expect a second chance if you're wrong. "We guard against sensationalizing or exaggerating the implications of the stuff we're exposing constantly," he insists. "We have a standard rule, for example, that on every story I break I must call the accused person first and include his explanation or refusal to comment. Also, we're leery of allegations from persons whose emotional stability we suspect—we get a lot of these kinds of situations, too."

Equally important, though, is the strong support he gets from corporate officers of the Charleston *Gazette*. "My publisher is gung-ho for tough exposés," he adds with a quiet confidence. Like others in the field, he believes such backing is vital. "I never think much about shield laws really. When I get potent information from an apprehensive source, I always promise that I'll go to jail before I reveal his identity, and I'm prepared to. It hasn't happened yet, but I once had a grueling afternoon before a county grand jury when I refused to identify a source."

Jim believes investigative reporters must maintain communication among themselves. Consequently, he supports an effort by Indianapolis *Star* reporter Harley Bierce to establish the Investigative Reporters and Editors Group, a loosely structured association, created to provide services to those involved in such work. "It's really a way to establish some sort of clearinghouse for info so investigators around the country can get quick access to scandal backgrounds on promoters who move into our areas or businessmen who become involved with our political officials, etc.," he explains. "The group hopefully will publish a directory of investigators at all newspapers so we'll know whom to call for data from any locale. It should work quite well for all of us, considering our need for ready and reliable information. When I get a call from an out-of-state paper seeking info about some Charleston figure, I'm glad to cooperate because it usually means a good story for me on what the guy's doing in his new location."

His sources index on prominent West Virginians is impressive, colleagues claim. He has mined a motherlode among Charlestonians willing to talk about people who have abused public trust. He has witnessed some instances himself. For example, one of his first stories dealt with a Charleston street commissioner who had on-duty city workers busy building his private stone lodge. Haught and a *Gazette* photographer hid in the woods with telephoto cameras to record the construction of the commissioner's hideaway. The city official was dismissed and convicted as a result of the story. A short time later, Jim won a National Headliner Award for an exposé that stopped a $3 million pyramid sales promotion scheme in Kanawha County. This exposé eventually led to a prison term for the promoter. It was a Haught story, too, that let West Virginia readers know that a strip-mining firm owned by one of the state's four congressmen had destroyed the site of a valuable 300 A.D. prehistoric ruin.

A 1973 story sent two siding salesmen to prison, after Jim discovered their sales pitch was better than their performance. The piece also won him the first annual $1,000 consumer writing prize of the National Press Club. A more dangerous investigation emerged when he followed up a tip about vice in the city. His stories helped convict a Charleston policeman. They brought countercharges, too. The *Gazette* was sued for $14 million.

A typical day for Haught starts slowly and builds momentum during the afternoon and evening hours. "I get up at seven about every morning, fix breakfast for my four kids, plus a teenager who lives with us, plus two neighbor kids, and take them all to school," he says. "Then I putter around the house, drink plenty of coffee, read the newspapers, make some phone calls, and take off for the office about noon. Working for a morning paper does change your lifestyle somewhat. My wife keeps the kids the rest of the day.

"I work afternoons and evenings, strictly on my own schedule—I generate ideas and follow up on others—with no supervision really to speak of. I report directly to the publisher who leaves me mostly on my own . . . except when I'm trying to avoid a job assigned me; then he won't let me slough it off. I come and go at the office. A secretary takes my calls, so I'm not deskbound, thank goodness. In the afternoons, I tend to work more urgently on immediate daily copy, then in the evening I tend to putter with files and random phone calls and research."

While he attempts to separate his family life from his work, he's found, much to his chagrin, some of the subjects he's investigated have endangered the entire Haught household. Recently, during a dangerous period in a local investigation, a sheriff's deputy had to protect the family and residence because of threats. "But that was extremely rare," Jim adds quickly. Yet he does try to maintain a low profile and keep the family from unnecessary publicity because of his work. "I live in the woods, at a private lake, very wrapped up in my kids and their activities. After the stresses and conflicts and accusations I get daily doing most investigative pieces, I like to spend weekends walking in the woods, or taking the kids for weenie roasts or just sleeping out in a tent or on our floating dock. My wife, who used to work at the *Gazette*, takes some of my phone calls at home. Otherwise, the family is far removed from my job and work." Investigative reporting, he concludes, does attract loners. "At least that's true of me. Perhaps the isolated, alienated personality type is drawn because of the nature of the work. I really don't know."

And the future for Jim Haught?

"I don't see it as an editor . . . my personality just

isn't oriented toward that. I guess I need more ego-tripping or something. The impact of breaking startling disclosures under my byline is still important to me. Administrative work and even straight reporting seem less exciting. I'm rather lone-wolfish . . . and I'll probably remain so."

Photo of Seymour Hersh courtesy of the New York *Times*.

11

Sy Hersh:
The Hottest Property
in Washington

No matter what he does, Sy Hersh is going to be disliked—hated, in fact—by some. Perhaps he's interviewed them ("He calls at all hours and tries to trick you, get you mad or scare you"). Perhaps they're just readers ("He virtually ripped up the American military to get his big story") and they don't like what he writes.

But, without question, Sy Hersh has had a real impact on the field of investigative reporting.

"He's been the hottest property in D.C. in recent months. He broke the CIA stuff, leading to the creation of the Rockefeller and congressional inquiries. Hersh is also one of the most controversial newspaper reporters around, according to what I've heard of him. Some say he's as tough as some of his sources," says a Washington reporter.

New York *Times* investigative reporter Seymour Hersh, a one-time wire service staffer in Pierre, South

Dakota, and a former press secretary to Eugene Mc-Carthy, has no illusions or pretentions about who he is or what he does. Investigative reporting? "What a lot of crap . . . this mythology grows up around everybody and we've been corrupted, too," he fires back. He hates pomposity and portentousness.

"Everyone's suddenly discovered the quote unquote investigative reporter. It's probably not all that nice. Look what I do for a living, I expose things. The big thing is, just as we didn't want Nixon imposing his order on us, I don't think anyone wants newspapers imposing their version of order on the world either. If it's going to be up to the newspapers to control things we're all in trouble; because we're not that good, we're not that honest, and we're not really that skillful and we don't have that much integrity. So, you know, we're not that much like heroes really."

Those who know him and are familiar with investigative reporters would probably agree with a remark he made to a journalism student in upstate New York who called him to get his reactions to an assignment she was working on. "I'm just a reporter. I have breakfast with my kids (Matthew and Melissa) and come to work just like everybody else."

Yet he's a different breed of reporter, says Joe Eszterhas in a *Rolling Stone* interview. "Hersh is a hurricane of a man who seems to approach life as if it were a battlefield. He walks and talks like a speed freak but the energy is all natural; he doesn't even smoke. He devotes as much nervous energy in his tipsters (even the ones who call about flying saucers) as he does to helping his seven-year-old son find his Monopoly cards. . . . He is not much of a party-goer but spends a lot of time reading, and his reading is diverse."

One look at his credentials and you get the impression that this Chicago-born journalist was to his generation what Ben Hecht was to his peer group four decades ago. While some believe his book *Chemical Biological Warfare: America's Hidden Arsenal* (1968) played a role in this country's decision to stop producing biological weapons, it was MyLai 4, the story of a military massacre in 1970, that earned him a Pulitzer. He's also won two George Polk awards, a Sigma Delta Chi Distinguished Service award, and a number of other honors. The recognition has been well deserved considering the investigations he's launched. The N.Y. *Times* has carried his pieces about former Secretary of State Henry Kissinger's wiretapping of his aides; the Defense Department's theft of Kissinger documents; the secret bombing of Cambodia and North Vietnam; the CIA and its involvement in Chilean President Salvador Allende's overthrow and the agency's domestic spying. Although the *Times* followed the Washington *Post*'s lead in Watergate coverage, Hersh, who was pulled off another assignment, was producing four stories a week during the climactic days of 1972–73.

It was MyLai, though, that taught Hersh that newspapers aren't always interested in really "hard" news. MyLai was a story of senseless slaughter of innocent civilians by American soldiers, and not too many editors or readers were ready for that.

"I knew that newspapers would probably be the last to believe MyLai. The story wasn't for a journal of opinion. It was hard news and had to be written as such. And media knew about the story, too, but they didn't tell it until after my stories appeared," Sy told an audience of professional journalists in 1974.

He had quit the Associated Press and was researching a book when he got a call one afternoon from a lawyer acquaintance. ("He didn't call me because we were buddies. He called me because he thought I could check it out," Hersh later told *Rolling Stone*.) The lawyer said there was a rumor around that the army planned to court-martial "some kid" for killing seventy-five civilians in Nam. The lawyer said he'd heard the soldier was being held at Fort Gordon, Georgia. It turned out to be a story the army certainly didn't want to talk about. Fort Gordon officials said no one was being court-martialed there. It took Sy two full days and twenty-five phone calls to newspapers and army posts to verify that the soldier was Lieutenant William Calley, Fort Gordon was the base, and the death toll was one hundred nine, not seventy-five. The rest is history.

Hersh used his much-used American Express card to travel fifty thousand miles in three months to talk with members of "Charley Company" and piece together his story. Then came the added shock: no one wanted to publish what he found. While newspapers later were willing to pay up to $1,500 for rights to each story, Sy couldn't find an editor during the winter months of 1970 who would promise much after they read it. A little known syndicate, the Dispatch News Service which distributed material to about fifty newspapers, gave him first publication rights. Even then, half of the syndicate's periodicals declined the first offer.

Did he feel his reporting of MyLai was a significant factor in changing the public's attitude toward the war?

Several opinion polls didn't think so and neither does Hersh. He believes his stories, in fact, may have helped make Calley an American folk hero and actually hardened readers' opinions about the war.

That doesn't bother the former Chicago police reporter. More important, Sy insists, is that the story was finally published. He had been a public information officer in the military service, and he knew some of the rationalizations and tactics the army might use to suppress the story. "One of the truths about MyLai is that the truth came from the bottom. I tend to believe a young captain before I believe a senior colonel. Just my personal feeling is that by the time one gets to be a colonel in the army he's practically a trained liar, a professional liar. The young people don't know about this whole situation but as far as someone shooting someone, the basics, the captain says 'yes' and the colonel says 'I have no such information.' "

How do you know whom to believe?

"That's just an instinct, who to believe and who not to," he explains. "There are just certain people who say things to me that I know aren't lying . . . when I quote a source it means I believe him to be telling the truth, not just quoting him accurately. But then I don't fool around with sources either. You don't lie to people. It's as simple as that. You just don't play games. I find most people want to talk. Find the right person and ask the right questions and a lot of times they give answers. Sure, nine out of ten say they don't know what you're talking about and hang up, but sometimes, sometimes they give answers."

Yet, some don't agree with Sy's methods of getting a story or writing it. "My main observation about investigative reporters, with the possible exception of Sy Hersh and the definite exception of Jack Anderson, is that they are not afraid to go back to the person or persons being charged with wrongdoing and getting their side of the story, if any. And they make sure the reply is included in the first, main story—not wait for a second-day reply story" says former editor-publisher of the Hartford *Courant*, Bob Eddy.

"You make a judgment. You use your instinct and common sense," Sy retorts, adding that he doesn't think about his role objectively although he's cast as a modern-day Clark Kent.

While he doesn't always trust administrators, generals, admirals, legislators and bureaucrats, he doesn't avoid them either when he goes after a story. For example, when he discovered Air Force General John D. Lavelle was the man responsible for ordering the unauthorized bombing attacks on North Vietnam, he wanted to interview him face to face. General Lavelle retired on orders from the White House after he was relieved of command of Air Force units in Southeast Asia. He's believed to be the first four-star officer in modern U.S. military history to have been nominated to retire at a lower rank—lieutenant general.

The story, Hersh claimed later, was pieced together item by item. First, he got a lead on the name of the executive officer who was with the general in Saigon. The aide gave him a telephone number in nearby Gaithersburg, an upper-middle class community of federal middle management and professional people, where Lavelle had an apartment. Then it was confrontation time. He told the general on the phone what he wanted and Lavelle agreed to meet him on the golf course the same day. Like most of his contemporaries, Hersh knows the best kind of interview is when the subject is doing something he enjoys in an environment where he can relax. The golf course was perfect. The trick was finding the right moment. Did the general and his sons who went along want to see a different kind of game? Golfing, fortunately, had been one of Hersh's talents during his preinvestigative years. His game was usually in the under-80s. Sy got them interested in his booming shots with a five-iron and how to fade and draw the ball.

An hour or so later over beers in the clubhouse, Sy continues, a retired general told how he had given orders for bombing runs without official approval from Washington. The admission was disturbing even to a veteran investigative reporter. But the story had to be told. Later, one of the general's sons wrote Hersh and complimented him for accurately telling his father's side of the controversy.

The approach was the kind few journalism schools teach. But then Sy didn't graduate from a journalism school. He didn't decide to become a journalist, in fact, until he was twenty-two; after he had graduated with a bachelor's degree in history from the University of Chicago and had tried law school. He dropped out of law to become a copy boy. "I'm certainly not a walking advertisement for a journalism school," he says, and his $30,000 to $35,000 salary offers some hope to the liberal arts graduate that journalism education isn't always needed. J-schools or departments, he believes, can teach style and polish a person's writing but they can't teach the aggressiveness or the perseverance it takes to get the truth.

Aggressiveness is merely one of the traits friends and competitors detect in Sy's volatile personality. A habitual night worker who handles most of his telephone calls at home from dusk until early morning, he can be loud, abrasive, and charming, members of the Washington press corps say, depending upon the moment and the need. "He can perform personality changes quite deftly, although he denies it," said one reporter who has observed the Hersh technique. "At times he can be engagingly witty and at others, absolutely threatening." The tactics, obviously, have been successful. It's the kind of sagaciousness some would have predicted for the onetime Chicago White Sox baseball fan who grew up in a family of four on Chicago's South Side where his father ran a neighborhood dry cleaning store.

His first news work was with the Chicago City News Bureau where he handled crime stories for six months. Sy spent the remainder of that year on active duty as an information officer with the U.S. Army at Fort Riley, Kansas. He returned to Chicago after finishing his military tour of duty and, after the City News Bureau decided not to take him back, he joined with a golfing buddy to start a weekly in southwestern Chicago.

A year later, dissatisfied with where he was going and what he was doing (he wrote much of the editorial content, sold ads, and even delivered the paper when newsboys didn't show up), Sy quit. Following a trip to California to visit his mother and relax on the golf course daily, he went back to Chicago job-hunting. United Press International was looking for a bureau chief-reporter in Pierre, South Dakota, and Sy was hired. Within a year, he had punched copy on teletype machines and covered the South Dakota Legislature. When he asked for a transfer to the UPI Washington Bureau—a much sought-after position—he was offered Omaha instead. Consequently, he quit once more and went back to Chicago seeking another job.

Unable to find work with Chicago newspapers, Sy walked into the Chicago Associated Press Bureau just after someone had quit. In less than a week he was handling the night radio wire for Illinois stations, rewriting and condensing twice the number of stories he had handled in South Dakota. In 1965, the Associated Press sent him to Washington where he later turned freelance and tried to exist by selling articles to the *New Republic, Ramparts,* and the *Progressive* and handling press relations work for presidential candidate Eugene McCarthy. He joined the New York *Times* Washington Bureau in 1972, the year his book on MyLai was published.

What are the dangers in using confidential sources and in the increasing popularity of investigative reporting?

"One of the problems, I think, inherent in the idea of turning two guys loose to investigate the highway department for two or three months and investing $25,000 is that they're going to come back with a story whether they have one or not. The hardest thing to do in any reporting is not write when you don't have a story." Yet, Watergate demonstrated how poor media practices had become, he insists. "Standards of investigative reporting fell on their ass in Watergate. Particularly when it came to sources or finding sources. If it weren't for those two guys in Washington (Bernstein and Woodward) we probably would have passed over it. I think that even in Washington an awful lot of reporters are content to be stenographers. Also, I think we need a lot more people with lot more smarts in the business; there are an awful lot of dumdums."

Hersh uses the telephone like an experienced surgeon uses a scalpel. He spends hours in the office and at home placing one call after another. The telephone, say reporters who have watched him work, is not really an instrument, it's more like a weapon. "He trades a piece of information for something else and begins to thread the story from call to call. He milks each for what it's worth and he usually gets people to say more than they think they're saying . . . his technique is to attack." Sy doesn't see it that way. "That's really ridiculous. You can't, really. The trick is to relax and be sort of funny . . . not intimidate or threaten."

The stony-faced *Times*man who likes to work with shirt sleeves rolled up, gets his share of hate mail, too. Yet he doesn't fear repercussions or bodily harm because of his stories. He insists he is apolitical—a neutrality that enemies and sources alike can live with. "Integrity and ethics are the vital elements really. I speak pretty freely but when I write, it's different. There are stories I haven't written simply because I couldn't prove them . . . even though I knew them or thought them to be true," he told *Rolling Stone* readers.

And what of the kooks who merely need a byline to set a senseless murder in motion whether it be reporter or personality?

"I don't have time to think about them."

Photo of Philip Meyer with his calculator and printouts as seen by his daughter, Caroline Meyer. Photo by Caroline Meyer.

12

Computers Turn
Phil Meyer On

Phil Meyer of Knight Newspapers is the scholar of the Washington press corps. While colleagues seek White House leaks and rumors and follow up on cabinet and congressional press releases much as their predecessors did two hundred years ago, he tells reporters to go buy slide rules because "journalism must become a social science in a hurry."

The advice, to some editors and reporters, is pure nonsense—"the kind of bunk some of these journalism schools are made of." However, a growing number of journalists have found the forty-six-year-old Washington correspondent's message is not radical; it's more a matter of common sense for the 1970s and 1980s. Phil describes his hypothesis in a 1973 book appropriately titled *Precision Journalism: A Reporter's Introduction to Social Science Methods.* The book, says Professor Hillier Krieghbaum of New York University in a review in *Edi-*

tor & Publisher, offers solid evidence that the author's premise is correct. It provides polls and surveys and explains the methodology (a term social scientists feel comfortable with) newspersons can use in gathering information while producing the kind of copy editors and publishers demand. In nuts and bolts language, Meyer talks about the mechanics of a new variation of investigative journalism.

"We journalists would be wrong less often if we adopted to our own use some of the research tools of the social scientists," he explains. "The tradition that the world of knowledge is populated by two different kinds of people—those who read and those who count—is swiftly decaying. Increasingly, it takes both skills to get along, and not just in the academic world. Public policy makers are learning to count and measure, or at least to work with people who do. This trend means that those of us who opted for verbal skills by taking up journalism have some catching up to do. The first step in catching up is to get rid of our natural fear of numbers. And the easiest way to do that is to go down to the dime store and buy a slide rule."

Of course, Meyer's contention strikes the middle-aged reporters and editors the hardest. It's new and something beyond the tools they acquired in college or on the job which have traditionally included a typewriter (which some are still trying to master), illegible note-taking, a memory (not always accurate but usually creative), not to mention stamina, guts, and initiative.

But investigative reporters know that his conclusions are as practical as the intuitive value judgments most used to gather information for investigative pieces. Says one newspaper executive who has observed Phil's techniques: "He's scholarly and reflective . . . a rare combination. He has specialized in recent years in using the disciplines of the sociologist and the statistician to get at complicated stories . . . and he's been most successful."

The slide rule, though, is merely one of the tools. The computer is another. Some frown upon the highly impersonal data processing equipment for frequently spewing forth far more than necessary. It produces irrelevant information, tons of it, and it's time-consuming, others insist. Not Meyer. Merely a matter of understanding, he says patiently. "He has taken the time to learn the uses of equipment others ignore because they don't know how to use it (or what it produces). More important, he strives to be more accurate while others are willing to risk preciseness for more colorful accounts," says a colleague. A few believe he is just fascinated by gadgets. And they're probably right.

At a workshop on investigative reporting at the University of Florida in 1973, he startled traditional journalists when he showed up with a computer terminal in a suitcase and let guests sample its resources (he plugged a telephone into a special receptacle on the terminal and dialed the Dartmouth College Computer Center in Hanover, New Hampshire). He talked about dealing with the growing amounts of computer data. "Computers are indispensable when the information available is disorganized or there's far too much to conduct analysis," he told Southern journalists.

What kind of satisfaction does he get from investigative work?

"A sense of personal efficacy," he explains. "I know it sounds selfish, but that's how it is." His definition of rewarding investigative assignments can take either of two directions, narrow or broad forms.

"If you are using the narrow version," he continues, "putting somebody in jail, getting somebody out, uncovering individual wrongdoing, etc., it would be my pieces on school insurance and political patronage in Dade County, Florida, in 1959 while I was a reporter on the Miami *Herald*. If you will accept a broader definition of investigative reporting, then I have to nominate the 1967 Detroit riot project (a post-riot survey of blacks in Detroit) ; a social science type of survey of the riot area done on newspaper deadlines. I liked the former because it was then that I first realized that what a reporter does makes a difference; and the latter because it demonstrated that research tools not previously thought of as being available to reporters were indeed available, and the profession was capable of development."

Detroit was the kind of challenge Meyer relished. The scene looked like Berlin just after the war, observers said. A routine police raid on an after-hours watering hole, and suddenly fourteen square miles of the inner city ignited during the final week of July causing an estimated $250 million worth of damage. Forty-one people died in the racial warfare that followed as snipers and bricks pelted predominantly white rescue units and firefighters who attempted to help people or property. Working out of the Knight Newspapers' Detroit *Free Press*, Phil sifted and sorted through data in the weeks after the riots to find answers to questions like the one then Governor George Romney asked of anyone in sight as he poked through ashes with a police guard at his side: "Who's going to rebuild this place after the troops go home?" The Washington Bureau reporter's series helped Detroiters find explanations and seek answers.

Meyer led a survey team into the inner city that interviewed hundreds of residents. The team culled the results and selected a portion for further exploration—indepth analysis. The data were fed to computers for response evaluation. The reporters interpreted the qualitative printout and wrote the series "The People Beyond

12th Street," a study of the July 1967 riot. It was one of the few reportorial race relations newspaper articles praised by Chairman Otto Kerner's Report of the National Advisory Commission on Civil Disorders.

"The neat thing about the project," Phil recalls, "was the way the crisis situation inspired people to such tremendous effort. The *Free Press* had no money for a survey, but Managing Editor Frank Angelo tapped some local donors and arranged for the work to be done under the auspices of the Urban League. Some of his other community contacts led us to the cadre of school teachers who served as interviewers. We were able to keep an amazing number of operations going at once—sampling, training interviewers, writing the questions—by tapping resources within or easily available to the newspaper, proving that very large obstacles can be overcome when the situation calls for it."

The twenty-five all-black interviewers had a significant and, at the same time, delicate role. They had to use a generally phrased question much like the one used in the UCLA survey of the Watts neighborhood after the rioting which revealed the person's involvement in the disturbance. "Would you describe yourself as having been very active, somewhat active, or slightly active in the disturbance?" they asked. The interviewer had to convince his respondent that involvement in a riot wasn't necessarily seen as abnormal behavior.

Twelve days later on a Saturday night, two key punch operators, moonlighting for the *Free Press*, transcribed the data onto cards. The next day, an off-duty programmer built a taped data file from a stack of 1,311 cards—three for each of the 437 interviews. The IBM 360/40 hummed a response; first a tabulation of the data and then a second pass to crosstabulate all of the variables in the responses and test the significance of the findings. The results? More than four hundred pages of output which gave solid evidence about the differences among rioters.

"One of the most vivid memories I have is the line of copypersons slowly circling a table in the city room, collating the questionnaires on the night before we entered the field. I've run a lot of surveys since then, but never at anything like that speed, the adrenalin flow evidently having peaked that time in Detroit," Phil says, reconstructing that hot summer.

For the newsman, Nebraska-born, Kansas and North Carolina-educated (B.S., Kansas State, 1952; M.A., North Carolina, 1963), the development was also a natural extension of his curiosity, practical news background, and the frustration that comes from the realization that new ideas take time.

He started his newspaper career on the Topeka daily *Capital* shortly after graduating from KSU. But he found he needed more expertise and he returned to academe—this time North Carolina, where he was a graduate assistant and instructor—and he spent two years finishing his course work (he received his degree after completing his thesis in 1963). In 1958, he joined the Knight Newspapers in Miami. Four meteoric years later, he was named to the Washington Bureau and, with the exception of one year on leave at Harvard as a Nieman Fellow, he's been with Knight ever since.

His efforts have won awards, too. Phil's 1959 pieces on political patronage in Dade County earned him the Public Affairs Reporting Award from the American Political Science Association. But awards weren't what he was seeking. His self-analysis detected flaws. For example, he was so embarrassed after he predicted eventual losers would be winners in two Ohio elections (he traveled the length and breadth of the state to conduct his surveys), he wrote to Harvard to implore the Nieman Fellowship

Committee to give him a year's study so he could find his mistakes and correct them. The social science he knew in college during the 1950s had changed, he admitted. At Harvard he took undergraduate courses in statistics and computers to better understand the change. In an article for the *Nieman Reports* he predicted that the journalist must master the social scientist's tools if his credibility is to be retained. "Precision Journalism" was a product of the Harvard experience. In 1974, it won the Sigma Delta Chi book of the year award.

At a point in his career where many have talked of managing or owning their own publication, Phil is still more interested in the results of his work than the acquisition of property or profits. "If I aspire to anything," he says, "it is to be publisher or maybe editor and publisher. I want what I do to matter though. Why else do anything? A publisher can make a difference by the examples he sets. A reporter can make a difference by the consciousness he creates or inspires. I've done the latter, may still be doing it now and then, so my aspirations are pretty much fulfilled at this stage in my career."

But his lifestyle as a reporter is different from that of other investigative newspeople. It lacks the excitement of reporters like Pam Zekman of the Chicago *Tribune* who changes identities to meet the new assignment, or Nick Gage of the New York *Times* who spends his day cradling a telephone. It has its own pace—its own purpose. "For the past few months, for example, I have been detailed to marketing problems," Phil explains. "If a man is really good at getting answers to inscrutable problems he ought to be of some help on the business side, too." The pace, though, would be considered leisurely by some of his colleagues.

"Today, I was awakened by WETA-FM—Bill Cerri playing Haydn—had my Alpen cereal for breakfast, sprinted two blocks to catch the commuter bus, read

Merle Miller's book on Truman, picked up the morning mail, and spent some time with the *Wall Street Journal.*" He then went to work on the market research project for one of the Knight papers. But there were interruptions— some pleasant, some distracting—before he finished his day. "I advised a younger colleague in the bureau on a survey he was conducting and advised a colleague my own age on a survey he was interpreting. In the afternoon, I consulted with an editor on a possible summer intern with a social science background and I reported to a superior about the status of an incipient project for correlating campaign contributions with roll call votes in Congress." By now, it was late afternoon. After helping the next-to-youngest member of the bureau celebrate his birthday, Phil took a short nap and caught the bus home.

Although the Meyer home on Kalmia Road in northwest Washington poses totally different kinds of situations for a veteran newsman, the pace remains about the same. "I gave my oldest daughter (Phil and Mary Sue have four daughters) permission to visit her boyfriend, opened the American Express bill, listened to a new Herbie Hancock album I just bought, set the timer on the clock-radio for 6:40 and retired."

But it's much different when he's working on an investigative project. Like other investigative reporters whose work consumes weeks and months instead of 8-to-5 days, Phil tries to keep his assignments and family separated "like church and state; watertight compartments. If ways rise for them to share in some success I have had, we take advantage of them. Most often this takes the form of another member of the family, Mary Sue or one of my daughters, traveling with me on a business trip, for example, a research project, a convention, or a speaking engagement. But I do not, could not, will not talk about my work at the breakfast table. One of the reasons for having a home, I feel, is to be able to step out of the other role. You need a place to which to step."

And how does Phil Meyer see Phil Meyer?

A person who has acquired more control with age; one whose age and circumstances have brought inevitable changes. He has witnessed the transition realistically, not fatalistically, and he recalls the evolution. "As a young reporter in Miami, I fraternized almost exclusively with other newspaper types—reporters and editors. It was the professional thing to do. The social and economic distance between me and other interesting people in town was too great. I wasn't about to fraternize with news sources."

And now? "Obviously, I'm more affluent, mobile, and connected to the social networks of other professions; and the connection is not one based on a reporter-source relationship either. So I see relatively fewer fellow journalists than when I was younger."

Associates say he's not the kind they would characterize as introvertive and Phil agrees emphatically. "That's something I'm definitely not—I ain't a loner."

Photo of Tom Miller courtesy of Huntington (West Va.)
Herald Dispatch.

13

To Tom Miller,
His Home Is His Office

"I'm a loner in my office, I guess, mostly because I spend as little time there as possible. I sense resentment from some colleagues because of my freedom of movement and total lack of daily beat assignments. Not really that many people in the office I want for friends, though. My friends come from outside the business...."

Lanky Tom Miller pushes his glasses back self-consciously as he describes himself and his relationship with reporters and editors at the Huntington Publishing Company, Huntington, West Virginia, where he has worked for seventeen years. The thirty-six-year-old investigative reporter has watched colleagues become editors, move on to larger papers, or find success in other careers. But it doesn't faze him a bit.

"Gee, in the next ten years, I may realize my dream and really become a hermit. Probably I'll be doing pretty much the same thing as I am now," he muses. "The same thing I've done really since I joined the paper in 1958 as a reporter. I may find at forty-six that I want a soft desk job, though. Right now, however, I think I may well be happy in 1985 doing exactly what I'm already doing. I definitely feel I would prefer to be doing reporting in West Virginia rather than New York City, Chicago, or even Atlanta."

No wonder. Tom has selectively mined important investigative pieces the length and breadth of the hilly, mineral-rich state. And his work has received the praise of colleagues in the state and nationally. In 1975, for instance, he received two national awards for a sensitive probe of absentee ownership and taxation of the state's land and mineral resources. Some prominent West Virginians were uneasy about his stories; others incensed. The series "Who Owns West Virginia?" was published in the Huntington *Herald-Dispatch* in December 1974, the culmination of the newspaper's year-long investigation of coal issues, and it stimulated legislative interest in reform of taxation of coal-producing land. Not long ago, he completed an eight-part series (due in part to reader inquiries) on "Who Owns West Virginia Media?" The articles silenced a widely held misconception in the Mountaineer state about collusion between big business and the media. While few financial data were available, he discovered that out-of-state interests have not dominated West Virginia media (nineteen of twenty-nine dailies in the state are owned by residents).

He won the Gerald Loeb Award, described by its sponsor, the Graduate School of Management, University of California at Los Angeles, as the "Pulitzer Prize for business and financial writing" for his work on coal issues. He also won the John Hancock Award for excellence among newspapers with less than 100,000 circulation for the 1974 series. Sponsored by the John Hancock Mutual Life Insurance Company, this award encourages lucid reporting and interpretation of business and financial news.

Tom's carefully researched pieces about his state's leading industry—coal-mining—and the politics surrounding it impressed awards panel judges. "Without question it was the most rewarding piece I've worked on," he notes with satisfaction. "It had statewide ramifications, apparently helped prompt important legislation during the 1975 legislative session and it shows promise of more stories. But most important, I believe, it has opened up many other leads to me from people now acquainted with my work on this. And, hopefully, it may even help in some small way to correct some of the present problems in this resource-rich, yet poverty-stricken state."

It was the kind of investigation that Miller wanted to do from the time he sat in Professor W. Page Pitt's reporting classes at Marshall University in the late 1950s. A journalism major, Tom was a quiet, smiling type, classmates said, possibly the antithesis of the aggressive reporter stereotype of the day. But he was ambitious, persistent, and more determined than his friends realized. He kept after *Herald Advertiser* Sports Editor Ernie Salvatore for work, and finally got a job on the sports desk a year before he received his B.A. from Marshall. His first four years, in fact, were spent handling sports assignments for the *Advertiser,* the afternoon daily in Huntington. In 1962, he moved to city hall and general assignment. Four years later, Tom was assigned to cover the West Virginia Legislature in Charleston.

His most significant reportorial change came in 1972, though. After fourteen years with the *Advertiser,* Tom moved to HupCo's morning paper, the *Herald Dispatch,* where he was given the opportunity to concentrate on politics and investigative reporting. His knowledge of the Huntington area and West Virginia politics made him the ideal choice of editors. With a variety of sources cultivated over the years and management's support, he began zeroing in on problems he had watched develop. And results came relatively soon. In 1974, Tom and reporter Sherrie Moran were awarded second place in the annual West Virginia State Associated Press Contest for outstanding stories. The Huntington team exposed fake sales of merchandise to the Cabell County Commission. At the same time, his series "Who Owns West Virginia?" had already stirred so much interest at the end of the year that he won first place in the AP contest for reporting without a deadline.

Tom doesn't deny that national recognition and the money that goes along with it (the Loeb and Hancock awards were worth $1,000 each) are certainly inviting. But he insists the satisfaction that comes from investigative reporting still offers more excitement and challenge for him than any other journalistic task. "It is a generally complete work," he says of investigative projects, "whereas day-to-day reporting is often so fragmented. In investigative reporting, you tackle a subject, you check and recheck and you ultimately put your tit in the wringer because even your editor has to have confidence in you and rely on your information, your thoroughness, and your judgment. That's why I prefer it." And because his instincts—like those of a beat cop—are still in reporting, his goals are different from those of others his age. "The power of the press, overestimated by some and underestimated by others, is in the day-to-day contact with people—not in the office staff meetings. Editors perhaps have the prestige but there is no real money in journalism at virtually any level. The editors I know handle a lot of paperwork, attend countless two- or three-hour meetings all day, and seem to be mostly frustrated reporters, so they write dull weekly columns, etc., to make up for it. I'm a reporter and I like it that way."

While his schedule is dictated by the work load he imposes upon himself, Tom's day is hardly the norm for a general assignment reporter. A single entry during the month shows why: "I got up about 8:30 and spent an hour or so reading our morning paper to check on developments I didn't get a chance to see the night before. I had my usual cups of coffee. Drove to the state capital, fifty miles away, to finish some daily legislative work I had to do, and then stopped to talk with at least three state officials about potential stories. I stay in touch as often as I can when I'm at the capital so they remember me. I checked back in my office in Huntington late in the afternoon for meetings to map my tentative work schedule for the next four months. I wrote three daily stories, which wasn't unusual for me up until recently, and then I learned I was officially free to work whatever hours each week I chose (actually I had been doing that for years unofficially). I arrived home for dinner with the family about 7:30 P.M. No sooner had I sat down to eat than I got a call from Phoenix, Arizona, from a private detective to arrange an appointment for the following day to discuss a story he had kept me posted on for six months. This too resulted from the series on who owns West Virginia and it may be a real good story on land speculation in West Virginia in months ahead."

Tom's best working hours would probably disappoint the sophisticate who argues that the Clark Gable "Front Page" image of newspapering is ancient history.

"I am finding more and more that I prefer to work— that is, type out my first drafts of stories—at home between 11:00 P.M. and 4:00 A.M. with my faithful bottle of Kentucky bourbon. The house is not large enough for me to have a secluded place, so I wait until the family is asleep. My wife says she can always tell when I am working on an involved story project because I never really seem to be listening when she talks to me. The actual writing, though, should be a piece of cake if you did the research correctly."

Yet, like others who desire family life and try to blend it with work that demands long hours and mental and physical stamina few people possess, Miller tries to keep his wife and sons with him wherever possible. "I sometimes take the family with me on trips when it's practical, because I'm away from home so much. Frankly, that's the one feature I don't care about in this work. My family is generally interested in what I'm doing and I try to keep them posted as much as possible. With others, I draw the line. I don't talk of my projects with friends or neighbors, etc."

Although he's convinced that investigative journalism will grow, perhaps prosper, Tom is less sure that those who champion protection for the investigative reporter are going to aid the field. And he's worried about those who attempt to popularize the notion that there is a need for more investigative efforts each year.

"I don't favor a shield law because I don't feel it would be that effective. I don't know of any good reporters that do, in fact. I suppose, though, there are some," he responds when the question is asked. "Responsibilities of the investigative reporter, I believe, are to the reader and the management he works for and they certainly are no different than those of other reporters. The point is, as a reporter, you get it right, get it first, and get it good. The primary concern is always the individuals who may be criminally, ethically, or morally involved in the investigation. Even if they are outright scoundrels, you wonder about their family, friends, etc. And that puts pressure of a different kind on you. There is always a nagging fear there is some stone you didn't turn that may come back to haunt you."

A bigger concern, he insists, is that some newspapers may "overdo investigative efforts. You can't create stories of this kind—they are either there or they are not. I am not a twelve-month investigative reporter. I cover legislature, state government, and investigate when there is a legitimate investigative story to do. Regardless of the pressure, we have to remember there is no Watergate every year. The toughest thing I face now is my thought that I should be able to come up with something this year or next that is as good or better, in my mind, than what I did last year. Can I top what I did on the 'Who Owns West Virginia?' series? I don't know. I know that it doesn't really happen that way every year."

Photo of Clark R. Mollenhoff by Jens Gunelson.

14

Clark Mollenhoff:
An Energetic Bulldog
With a Bite

National correspondent Mollenhoff of the Des Moines *Register* and *Tribune* has strong opinions about his field and the people in it. And he doesn't hesitate to expound.

At a Boston University School of Public Communications seminar not long ago, the vocal Iowa native told an audience that reporters have, for too long a time, been "too respectful. . . . I can count on two hands the number of reporters willing to do any work."

A year or so earlier at a Nieman Convocation on media and government, the bearish-looking six-foot, four-inch, national columnist, whom some call the dean of the Washington investigative journalism corps, bluntly challenged a number of his colleagues who supported a shield law.

"I've spent twenty years on this subject and think that I know it pretty goddamn well; and I'm amazed at some of the juvenile amateurs who are in the investigative field for one or two shots who take the other position. I'm sympathetic with them in not wanting to go to jail, but I'm also sympathetic with all the people who don't want to go to jail. There are newspaper reporters as well as other citizens who deserve to be in jail, not necessarily because of the wrong they have done, but in such cases as the Bridge case [Peter Bridge, a former reporter for the Newark, N.J., *Evening News* was jailed for refusing to reveal a source—see chapter 4] and the Farr case [Bill Farr, a former reporter for the Los Angeles *Herald Examiner*, has fought litigations since he refused to give a county court judge his sources for a story in the Manson-Tate murder case] because of the utter stupidity with which they arrived at the decision to go with the stories in the manner in which they handled them. . . . My experience with the press is that there are a few people in our ranks whose motives are not quite balanced all the time, and I think that's putting it mildly. There are some people in our ranks who are irresponsible."

The comments help describe his attitude toward investigative reporting. "This is a rough game, and it takes a tough participant, and its been that way all the time. It is always going to be that way," he insists.

Few newspapermen have been able to outmanuever or "out-tough" the Pulitzer-prize winning reporter from Burnside, Iowa. "Clark is a bulldog and his law degree (Drake, 1944) has helped him immensely in seeking his facts," says Bob Eddy, former editor and publisher of the Hartford *Courant* and a long-time friend. "Clark, of course, was one of the first, one of the best, and surely one of the most persistent and courageous," a press association official adds. "He has a superabundance of energy and he works at a feverish pace."

Others, especially the younger members of the Washington press corps, are more critical. "Clark isn't my kind of writer. I'm told, he often needs editing. But he is and always has been an insatiable inquirer and digger. He is also aggressive, which it often takes to get such information. He has become somewhat of an establishmentarian. Perhaps the Nixon White House stint did that to him. You really don't hear as much about the Des Moines Washington Bureau as you used to. I can't recall anything spectacular that it has done recently. I know his bureau didn't do anything great during the Watergate affair," says a young reporter in a Washington Bureau of a major Midwestern daily.

The fact remains that Clark Mollenhoff, captain of the Drake University football team, Nieman Fellow, Navy officer in the South Pacific, special counsel to President Richard Nixon, former Washington Bureau chief, author of seven books, and journalistic prizewinner, still has an abundance of "clout" with the Washington press corps. He's known as a bold decisionmaker who thrives on pressure and relishes controversy.

When Watergate shoved other matters from the front pages, Clark and reporters George Anthan and James Risser were preoccupied with an investigation of scandals and mismanagement in the regulation of international trading in grain and domestic trading in commodities and livestock. Like other newsmen at the time, they tried to pursue Watergate leads but they didn't lose sight of their own investigation. "Watergate quite naturally dominated the national scene," said the late Jack Bell, a long-time Washington reporter for the Associated Press and later, Gannett Newspapers. "But it's also obvious that Clark's work on the grain scandals and government mismanagement in agricultural affairs was of great importance to Iowa readers, too."

The significant developments on the grain trading investigation occurred from August 1974 to August 1975. The preliminary research, however, covered three years,

Clark said. "The coverage was divided into three general categories: (1) exposure of laxity, mismanagement, and corruption in the grain inspection system and irregularities and problems in the international grain trade; (2) exposure of laxity, mismanagement, and corruption in the control and regulation of the $500 billion a year trading in commodities under the old Commodity Exchange Authority; and (3) exposure of laxity and mismanagement in the administration of the Packers and Stockyards Act that permitted frauds against livestock producers and anticompetitive practices in the feeding and sale of cattle, hogs, and broilers."

A seven-part series in the *Register* and *Tribune* in March 1975, which examined in more detail issues and allegations in earlier articles, brought legislative action. Federal personnel responsible for mismanagement and laxness were fired or suspended, criminal prosecutions were sought, the administration of the laws was tightened, and bipartisan support was given to proposals to establish more direct federal control over the system after the Senate and House conducted their own investigations.

Earlier, a new Commodity Futures Trading Commission Act of October 1974 established an independent five-member commission to regulate the commodity markets after examining the inequities of the old Commodity Exchange Authority. Senate and House committee reports in 1974 and a General Accounting Office report in June 1975, verified the basic findings of two *Register* stories that urged passage of legislative reform.

The *Register* series in the spring of 1975, moreover, caused bipartisan congressional support for sweeping amendments to the fifty-four-year-old Packers and Stockyards Act. These included a plan to bring the nation's packers under the bonding provisions for the first time. And senators and representatives, normally reluctant to credit others for their positive legislation, praised the *Register* investigative team for their work. Said Senator Dick Clark (Rep., Ia.), one of the Senate authors: "The initial impetus for this legislation came from the ... series in the Des Moines *Register* last year (1973) on a particular example of abuse arising from the lack of effective regulation...." A month later, Representative Neal Smith (Dem., 4th Dist. Ia.) a House co-author told his colleagues: "I compliment the (Agriculture) committee for relatively speedy action and also give credit to some investigative reporting by Des Moines *Register* reporters who helped expose and interpret the very complicated situation. As the gentleman (Chairman Poage) said, we only last week saw what could have been a manipulation as a result of sale to a foreign country. The same thing could happen at any time in those commodities which are now in short supply. We need this legislation and the protection it provides as soon as possible." The reporting, Mollenhoff maintains, was one of the *Register*'s best all-around efforts in Washington.

When he is asked about rewarding investigative projects, Clark vividly recalls episodes and incidents that span over twenty-five years from the Midwest to Washington. "The most significant? The local police scandals in Des Moines and Polk County, Iowa, in the 1941–1950 period. The work was done alone, or only with a few people, and it was possible to have the total grasp and to have immediate impact and results. I got the Nieman Fellowship in 1949–50."

After studying governmental administration and the history of American government at Harvard while a Nieman Fellow, Clark accepted a position as Washington correspondent with Cowles Publications, writing and investigating government operations and related stories for the *Register,* Minneapolis *Star,* and *Tribune* and for *Look* magazine. "I've enjoyed in some degree my role in

investigating federal government corruption and mismanagement from 1950 to the present. During the first
ten years I was involved in in-depth investigations of
nearly every government department and agency as well
as all six regulatory agencies, I suppose."

His accomplishments—seven award-winning investigative projects among the hundreds he has worked on in
Washington—rank him among the country's best.

During the early 1950s, he earned the Sigma Delta
Chi award for Washington correspondence for his stories
about the tax scandals in the Truman Administration. A
short time later, his probing articles about the Iowa "connections" to the crime syndicate investigation of Senator
Estes Kefauver's committee and several follow-through
pieces about the Dixon-Yates Project—the conflict of interest between public and private sectors involving control of utilities in Mississippi—established his name and
work as an investigative reporter.

The Wolf Ladejinsky security case, which surfaced
in 1954-55, brought him more recognition. He again won
the SDX Award for Washington correspondence, as well
as the Raymond Clapper and Heywood Broun Awards
among other honors following his stories about the Eisenhower Administration security leak. "This was as
much a one-man push as any I have been in in Washington," he says when he reminisces about the investigation.

Yet it was his inquiry and stories about Jimmy
Hoffa and his 1,500,000-member Teamsters Union that
gave him national prominence. Clark's persistence and
solid investigative effort helped create Senator John Mc-
Clellan's Committee on Improper Activities in Labor and
Management which, in conjunction with the AFL-CIO
Ethical Practices Committee, unearthed violations of
trust, corruption, and disregard of members' rights in
1957. He received the Pulitzer for national reporting and
the Sigma Delta Chi Public Service Award in 1958.

His tenacity has earned him the reputation as a fighter who is willing to take on bureaucrats and presidents. "The Adams-Goldfine case (Eisenhower aide Sherman Adams who received gifts from industrialist Bernard Goldfine and later resigned as a result of the controversy that evolved) was a total press corps project but I had some significant role in several important aspects. I had my third major confrontation with President Eisenhower on this matter including Adams' role and the use of executive privileges," he likes to remember. Clark won the John Peter Zenger Award from the University of Arizona and the Colby College Lovejoy Fellowship for his battle to open the Eisenhower Administration.

The fact is there haven't been many major investigative stories in Washington he hasn't written about or sought out his own sources to verify. The *Register* has carried his byline on stories about Bobby Baker, the TFX inquiry, and the Billie Sol Estes case, to name a few.

He's the kind of reporter who, although fiftyish with major accomplishments behind him, still needs no extra adrenalin to remain in a constant state of motion. His day is the kind of wearing, tearing scramble that many people try to escape, especially as they get older.

"I get to the office early—get on the telephone, write letters, and go to press conferences, to press cabinet officers and presidents if I can. The task is getting through the 'bureaucratise' to the meat of the discussion. I comb records and I try to stimulate various senators and congressmen to take on their responsibility and follow through. Yet I enjoy it all. The good days and the bad. It is all an important and essential part of getting the facts on mismanagement and corruption and calling it to the attention of the public and public officials ... and then, more important, getting something done about it."

He thought he could be of similar value when Richard Nixon invited him to join his administration in

1969. Clark saw it as an excellent opportunity to serve as an ombudsman. He described his disappointment in a *Register* and *Tribune* column a year later after he left government employment, discouraged and dazed by the daily frustrations and power struggles.

"Richard Nixon was bubblingly enthusiastic as I outlined the way a White House ombudsman could alert a president to budding scandals involving his subordinates. Then, in characteristic fashion, he took the initiative and explained to me what I had just told him, using President Truman and the Alger Hiss case as an example of a president who might have been saved a great deal of anguish had he been given all of the hard truths about the case at an early stage. 'It was the coverup that hurt,' Nixon said. 'It was inevitable that scandals would arise in any administration, but the secret is getting on top of all the facts at an early stage and cleaning them up.' ... The important thing to me was that he seemed to understand the corrupting influence of secret government decisions."

In the spring of 1970, after battling White House aides H. R. Haldeman and John Ehrlichman—the Berlin Wall, he called them—merely to get to see the president, Clark decided to resign. "I came to accept that the president either wanted it that way as a protective device or he was too weak and indecisive to break out of the 'Berlin Wall.' ... The Wall had seemed to grow stronger and more impenetrable every week. If the president didn't understand by then what the Haldeman-Ehrlichman control had done to his relationship with Republican leaders in the House and Senate, I felt it would be useless to tell him. ... As I left, he said he wanted to see me 'from time to time' to get my advice. 'If you see problems,' the president said, 'just tell Bob. He'll set something up.' "

Eager to get back into the Washington news scene, he was merely a phone call away from a job. Clark was the choice of the *Register* and *Tribune* management to head their Washington bureau and continue his work as an investigative reporter. Prior to his year's leave, he preferred to work alone and develop his own stories. His views have changed, however.

"I worked alone on many investigations because I felt I could do it best that way, or because there was no one available who had the kind of talent I needed. I have also worked with other reporters on a basis of sharing sources and story beats, and developed a team operation in our Washington bureau to deal with investigations. It has worked beautifully on the corruption and mismanagement in the commodity trading and similar kinds of probes."

Des Moines management, he says, gives him a free hand. "I have no complaints about the conditions we have. We have complete freedom to explore any area we want to explore that we feel might be productive and if we deal with it in a responsible manner there is no problem getting it into print with the facts. In return for this freedom we try to avoid irresponsibility in our treatment of our investigations, and any illegality in the development of the sources or evidence.

"From time to time, we may have differences with editors on the play a story is given, but we recognize that we are occasionally overly enthusiastic about our own stories because it is necessary to have a strong interest to do the job properly. Really, we need no help except the financing of the investigations we feel that should be done. We need no more protection than the continuation of the backing we have received and the encouragement of knowing that our editors like what we are doing. There's just never enough time to do all the things we would like to do though."

But the author of *Game Plan for Disaster,* his examination of the Nixon Administration, sees problems ahead for investigative reporting due, in part, to the popularity it enjoys today. "Solid investigative reporting has been with us for a long time and is a part of history of the best work in the search for truth, not just that little bit of truth that the politicians and business public relations people pour out. The current craze, touched off by the intense interest in the realities and the myths of Woodstein and Watergate, is a superficial faddist interest. It won't last, I believe. However, that faddist interest has created a new fascination with the techniques of investigative reporting as a serious profession, and that I have been dealing with in lectures at the American Press Institute over a period of the last twenty years. That serious professional interest has been increasing steadily and the magnificent job of twenty to thirty investigative reporters will keep the drama moving."

Part of the problem, he believes, is the professional manner in which a reporter handles confidentiality of sources. Some don't, he laments. "Confidential relationships will always depend upon a specific source and the specific reporter he's dealing with. There are a lot of reporters who, regardless of what they say, will be blabbermouths about what information they get and careless about the way they throw it around. But I have no problem at all. I find many injustices where I can go out and not only take the tip but put it together with the record, because I don't have to reveal my source—and that's the proper way to use it. You get a tip from any agency, somebody who knows what a situation is, and then you go out and try to put it together from the public sources—and then you go to the erring public official and ask him about it. That's the first thing you do in fairness anyway—you go to the public official you're going to charge, and then you rely upon the confidential thing only as a last resort. You don't even mention it in your story. But that's the problem: there are too damn many

people who want to say 'See, I got a confidential source!
I got a scoop!' "

Shield laws, which ostensibly would aid a reporter
in protecting sources, would give newsmen too much
power and invite irresponsibility, the lawyer-journalist
insists. "I am opposed to shield laws because they immu-
nize reporters from any accountability as much as 'executive privilege' would have immunized President Nixon.
Reporters who know their business seldom have problems
that would require a shield. Sources of a confidential nature are kept confidential and are not referred to in
stories under most circumstances. Confidential sources
of uncertain reliability must be corroborated in depth
and if this is done properly there is no need even to reveal
that one had a confidential source."

An absolute shield law, Clark told Wisconsin Congressman Robert W. Kastenmeier's committee hearings
on rights, would dilute the First Amendment. "Let's take
a look at what an absolute shield law is. That would
cover, as it should, everyone from pamphleteers to the
great press, to the great television networks. Remember,
the First Amendment was not written to cover just big
television and big newspapers; it's supposed to be for
those pamphleteers.

"Just from a practical standpoint," he said several
months later, "you are never going to get Congress to pass
a law that will provide a shield for your left wing, right
wing, fringe pamphleteers. . . . But when you examine
what it is, it would represent total coverage on all crime
from petty larceny up to murder and sabotage. It would
cover every forum from a county grand jury up to and including Congressional investigations. That's no different
from executive privilege.

"What an absolute shield law amounts to is an executive privilege for every reporter—cub reporter up to the
publisher. We've seen in the Watergate case what the ex-

ecutive privilege and the belief that they have a right to run behind the White House door and refuse to answer questions did to the Nixon Administration. And I had some considerable dealings with these people and understood from the outset the problem of where they were going to end up. Ehrlichman and Haldeman were not necessarily poorly motivated as they took the oath. They had this obsessive secrecy, they wanted to cover everything with secrecy. They permeated the White House atmosphere with that attitude and in the process corrupted themselves completely and corrupted the young men who were around them. I knew those young men and I had seen, I thought, the potential of those young men in 1969, and I saw what happened to them. . . . Executive privilege corrupted them. A shield law would corrupt the press just as much because secrecy is a corrupting influence. It's the greatest power that there is."

The courts, he adds, will be available to newsmen under circumstances where legitimate First Amendment interests require protection. "We're going to take it upon a case-by-case basis. I think that's where we should leave it."

Do his family and his wife Georgia share in his vicarious world of inside information about corruption within the federal bureaucracy?

"In a general way they know what I'm working on, except in a few rare instances," he says. "I don't bore them really with the details but I discuss the general thrust of the investigations and what I'm searching for, unless there is some peculiar reason for not discussing it." But the Mollenhoffs, their two daughters and a son, haven't had time to be bored; Clark's career has been a string of assignments stretching from Des Moines to Washington and spanning more than thirty years. And they've been in on each one.

Photo of Jack Nelson by R. L. Oliver of the Los Angeles *Times*.

15

Hassling Is a Way of Life for Jack Nelson

If there's ever an assemblage of the best of breed in investigative reporting, count on Jack Nelson to be there. Colleagues respect him; editors of competing papers grudgingly acknowledge his work; and those he's written about generally believe he's an honest journalist even if they hate him.

"Nelson is the type of guy who has been able to cultivate firsthand sources that slip him materials," says a Washington reporter. "He did this frequently during Watergate and during the House Judiciary Committee's impeachment inquiry throughout the summer of 1974. Jack has the clout of the third largest bureau in Washington to back him up, plus an influential congressional delegation. He's been around town long enough to build up the sources and the strength of the Los Angeles *Times* in cooperation with the Washington *Post* in a syndicate; those are the keys to his investigative work. He's a careful, patient reporter."

To those who knew him during the pre-Washington years, however, Nelson was a brash crewcut—some said arrogant—whose stories made him a marked man in several states.

He started investigative writing at eighteen—perhaps one of the youngest in the country at the time (the stories were called "depth" pieces then)—working in the Deep South during the preintegration days. He was a reporter for the Biloxi (Mississippi) Daily *Herald*. His investigation ripped the cover from gangland types and a few local residents who were handling gambling pay-offs and illegal slot machine concessions and operations. But the byline brought the kind of notoriety that intimidates, too.

By the time he reached twenty-one, he had been threatened with death at the bottom of Biloxi Bay. Three years later he found out that threats can become very real. While working on a series for the Atlanta *Constitution* about vice and corruption in Liberty County, Georgia, the energetic twenty-four-year-old played a major role in bringing indictments against twenty-two persons. When he showed up to cover the grand jury's findings, a six-foot five-inch, 250-pound deputy sheriff shoved him against the hood of a car in a parking lot, spreadeagled him in front of dozens of cheering bystanders ("Give the little bastard what he deserves," they shouted), and began choking him.

Somebody finally separated the two, and a town cop got Nelson out of the county with the warning that it would be healthier for Jack to stay in Atlanta. But the scrappy reporter—five-foot nine-inch and a lean 135 pounds—was enraged. He swore out an assault and battery warrant against the deputy and returned to take legal action. Southern justice, however, wasn't really equal in those days, regardless of race. The deputy brought a litigation against Nelson and in court the reporter was charged with trying to proposition bar girls. Both warrants were later dropped.

Jack knew, as other investigative reporters have ruefully discovered, when you hassle people you can expect plenty of hassling in return.

Occasionally, the hassle involves big stakes and powerful people. In 1970, for example, the Nieman Fellow wrote a story about the Federal Bureau of Investigation and the late J. Edgar Hoover that brought swift reaction. He had only been with the Washington Bureau of the Los Angeles *Times* a few months and Hoover appeared determined not to let such an upstart meddle with a federal law enforcement agency. The FBI director went to the Los Angeles *Times* general manager with a request: fire Nelson! A three-hour meeting with *Times* top management and later, a forty-five-minute session with Washington Bureau chief John Lawrence gave the aging FBI director no satisfaction. Hoover's reasons cast some doubt on his own credibility. Nelson, the FBI chief insisted, was a drunk who had run around Washington calling the director a homosexual.

There was little doubt that Hoover recognized Nelson as a threat to the bureau's traditional principle of secrecy. He probably knew that the reporter had contacts within his agency. Months later, the director knew for sure. Nelson's sources put him onto a story that the FBI had paid criminal informants $36,500 to set up two Ku Klux Klan hitmen in Meridian, Mississippi. Police and FBI agents caught the two—one actually was a woman—attempting to plant a bomb in a Jewish businessman's home. The woman was killed in the shootout. The setup had become, in fact, an execution.

None of those close to the case—the FBI, the Meridian Police, the Meridian Jewish community, or the Anti-

Defamation League—wanted the story published. Sources and officials persuaded Nelson that it would be in everyone's best interest if he dropped it.

Jack agonized over the decision. He had spent eight months digging up solid material on the case, yet he knew that he would lose some of his best sources, possibly for good, if the story was published. He worried about it, yet he also realized that published accounts gave the public little information to really understand what had taken place.

"I'd wake up in the night with knots in my stomach until it ran. I knew I'd lose sources. I didn't feel good about it but I knew I had to go ahead," he says today looking back.

The six-thousand-word story appeared in the Los Angeles *Times*.

The Meridian article introduced a situation Nelson hadn't faced before but, in retrospect, he believes he'd handle it the same way again. The situation? Paying sources for information. Jack agreed to pay a Meridian police detective $1,000 for a stack of records of meetings between the police and informants concerning KKK bombings in Mississippi. The detective, Jack later noted, had put in lots of time on the subject.

"There had been a series of seventeen unsolved bombings in Mississippi. The targets were mostly black, but two synagogues and a rabbi's house had been hit, too," he offers in defense. "The Mississippi Jewish community and the Anti-Defamation League went to the FBI, which said it needed money to pay informants. So, $78,500 was raised and paid to two informants who helped break the case. A Meridian detective was the chief negotiator and he wanted something out of it, too. He had the daily logs of the meetings and the *Times* authorized me to pay $1,000 for them. Ultimately, the detective sent the check back because of the pressure from the FBI."

Would he pay for information again?

Nelson has publicly said he would. "I'd be inclined to get together with the editors to see if we could work out something. It would [have to] be a matter of such overriding importance that I think it would be worth paying for the information."

Like the overwhelming majority of his peers, Jack likes to substantiate his stories with documents. He's realistic enough to know that sources don't always have access to printed materials, nor can he get hold of valuable papers without breaking laws. Consequently, he goes beyond most of his colleagues by asking his sources to sign sworn affidavits that the material they've provided is true. He has collected more than two hundred to date.

Times Assistant General Counsel Bill Niese echoes Jack's concern for accuracy. In a discussion of how the Los Angeles *Times* legal staff reviews investigative pieces before they are printed, Niese told members of the Urban Policy Research Council in Beverly Hills that there are certain do's and don'ts that must be observed. "One is that we try very hard to delete from the story any what I will call colorful words. We all like to turn a phrase, so to speak, to put a little sex appeal into these dry facts, and words like 'funnel' or 'bogus' or 'phony' repeatedly creep into the story.... They are colorful indeed but they add little to analysis and indeed confuse.... A second don't is keeping sources of possible libel suits to a minimum.... There is an inclination, a tendency among reporters to include in their article as much detail as possible for a number of reasons, most of which are proper from an editorial or reporting point of view.... I am simply saying that mentioning peripheral people is hazardous in the extreme and should not be done in these articles.... Peripheral people are a source of trouble. I think the last do and don't is attribute, attribute, attribute. It doesn't make sense not to attribute in such articles."

Jack has had his share of exciting stories, including a series in 1960 on a surgeon whose illegal practices he exposed, resulting in a Pulitzer Prize and a punch in the face. One assignment which he researched and wrote while on the Atlanta *Constitution* is still his most satisfying investigative piece.

"I'd have to say the series on Milledgeville State Hospital, Georgia, because it resulted in sweeping reforms and improvements in the treatment of the state's mentally ill," he says without hesitation. "When I wrote the series—and it continued over the better part of a year—the hospital was headed by a physician who was not a psychiatrist and who had certain problems of his own. With twelve thousand patients, Milledgeville was the second largest hospital in the nation. The state was paying only $2.42 per day for the care, housing, treatment, food, recreation, etc. of each patient. Purchasing scandals whittled that small amount down even further. The reforms included removing the hospital from the politically corrupt Welfare Department to the Health Department; bringing in a nationally known psychiatrist, Dr. Irving MacKinnon, head of Columbia University's Department of Psychiatry, as superintendent; increasing the budget by a huge margin; and the building of another mental health center in Atlanta. While I was satisfied with other pieces, I really felt good about this one."

Jack is an idealist when it comes to anticipated results of his investigative work, and he readily admits it. "I get the satisfaction of having what I always hope is a beneficial impact on the course of human events. That's very important to me. That may sound like a rather lofty ideal, but I do believe that responsible investigative reporting can influence the course of life for the better. I believe that. Some investigative stories result in punishment of the targets, of course. Politicians frequently are jailed or have their political careers ruined as a result of investigative reporting. And perhaps that's a wholesome result, too, but I get more satisfaction from more positive results, such as the Milledgeville case. I must say I did get satisfaction from exposing corruption in the Marion Griffin Administration in Georgia, 1955–58, because Griffin . . . had one of the most corrupt administrations in the state's history.

"For most investigative reporters, I suppose, there also is the satisfaction that frequently the things they do would not be done were it not for them. So there is a feeling that you are performing a worthwhile task that might not otherwise be done."

While his salary, which some associates place at $35,000, gives him a comfortable life, it doesn't begin to compensate him for the hours he spends weekly contacting sources ("I call up my contacts in Miami, Jackson, Mississippi, and New Orleans regularly just to chat"), researching, and writing.

His responsibilities have changed, too, since he joined the *Times* in 1965 as a special correspondent in the South. He's Washington Bureau Chief now. But administrative work is secondary to his reporting in many respects, he adds quickly.

"I accepted this job with the understanding that I would continue to do investigative reporting, which I'm doing in fact. I became bureau chief although I've never been ambitious to become an editor or a bureau chief for that matter. My ambition has been directed toward doing the very best I can as an investigative reporter. It was an opportunity that came my way because, said *Times* editors, they liked my approach to investigative reporting and appreciated the way I worked with other reporters in the bureau. I've always been strong on team investigative reporting when I felt it was warranted."

But the *Times* hasn't courted investigative writers over the years, nor has it nourished a tradition as a crusading newspaper. A conservative daily at the turn of the century, the paper was the scene of bitter battles and a bombing when typographers tried to unionize. The paper's management, the Chandler family, scorned the efforts of muckraker Lincoln Steffens who tried (and failed) to mediate the issue. Yet later generations of Chandlers have brought change to the *Times*. By the mid-1960s, young Otis Chandler had transformed the publication into one of California's best newspapers, said the London *Economist*. "A few years back it was a shoddy sheet of extreme right-wing viewpoint and a Hollywood divorce focus for its news measurement," the British periodical said in its review. And while it remains a Republican paper today—it supported Barry Goldwater in 1964 and both presidential bids by Richard Nixon—the *Times* has also crossed over to support other political candidates. In 1972, for example, the *Times* endorsed the campaign of black Democrat Tom Bradley against incumbent Sam Yorty for mayor of Los Angeles. The paper refused to support Gerald Ford or Jimmy Carter in 1976.

Circulation growth and continued review and change in its editorial stance and policies have made the daily successful. The *Times* is the country's third largest newspaper and one of the most profitable enterprises on the West Coast. Its editions are usually bulky (a definite sign of good health to publishers); on Sundays, it frequently offers readers more than two hundred pages. And its financial future is reasonably secure. The *Times* carries more advertising linage than any other newspaper in the United States.

At the same time, management has attempted to match its fiscal stability with respectability. Since the early 1960s, the paper has added eighteen more foreign correspondents and it enlarged its Washington bureau to four times its size shortly before Nelson joined the paper.

Jack's "typical" day as bureau chief has increased his tasks and hours rather than reduced them. He squeezes administrative duties between contacting sources and writing assignments. "There is no such thing as a typical day," he says. "Suffice to say that an investigative reporter's work is hardly ever done if he or she (and there are a few women now too) is really on a hot story. On routine days—both now and before becoming bureau chief—I come to the office around 9:30 A.M. and work until anywhere from 6:00 to 10:00 P.M. I spend a tremendous amount of time on the phone as well as pounding the pavement to talk to sources. Some of my best sources are other reporters, though, who know bits of information that may fit into a particular investigation I'm involved in."

While investigative reporters such as Nick Gage of the New York *Times* prefer to avoid crowds and work by themselves, Jack sees himself as an extrovert. "I've heard that some reporters are withdrawn but the description just doesn't fit me. On some cases I may work alone but I'm hardly a loner."

Yet he knows, as many successful reporters do, that the work requires a flexible personality that can exude friendliness, cloud up with abrasiveness, ask tough questions, and yet demonstrate genuine concern and compassion. It bothers him, but he accepts it as part of the job.

"People talk about excesses in investigative reporting and they are concerned that the reporter is becoming too glamorous. The investigative reporter has to be extremely careful and cautious, and he can't leave any questions unanswered. Why shouldn't a Rockefeller be questioned and examined (during the Senate's inquiry prior to his confirmation as vice president) about every detail of his public life? If he wants to be vice president let him stand up and take the investigations."

Unlike many of his Washington counterparts, Jack

takes his problems home quite frequently to talk over with his wife. But there aren't many Washington reporters' wives who hold equally important news positions either. Barbara Matusow Nelson is an NBC producer for WRC-TV Washington.

Jack has been in the field long enough to understand the hazards and obstacles that confront the investigative reporter, he says, but he believes that one must continue to take the risks. The reporter who rests on the successful completion of one story "will end up doing other things in time." Yet it's also true that the more successes one has, the more vulnerable he is in a city like Washington.

"One reason why many good reporters stay away from such work is they don't like hassling people nor do they want to be hassled," he admits. "That's the part of the job I don't like either, but I'm willing to put up with it because I believe such work is important. I don't like confronting government figures with the fact that they have lied about something or that they have done something irregular or illegal. It's an unpleasant experience. I don't particularly like the sneers I get back from such people. I don't like it that J. Edgar Hoover and other FBI officials tried to smear me as a drunk and a Jekyll-Hyde personality who was out to wreck the FBI. I didn't like it that Hoover told these things to my superiors. But I'm willing to put up with these things in the interest of my job."

Will shield laws provide investigative reporters with better protection and more latitude to obtain information?

"The only shield law I favor is one that is absolutely unqualified—that is, one which merely amounts to congressional sanction of the First Amendment right I think we already have to protect a source. . . . I don't care what material or what reporter it involves; if it involves a case where the government is trying to force someone to reveal his sources, I think he has a First Amendment right not to."

Yet while he staunchly defends the right to protect sources, his intuition and experience tell him that sources aren't always accurate either.

"If you place total reliance on every source you get, it could lead you to pretty sloppy and very dangerous kinds of reporting, too."

Photo of Gerard O'Neill courtesy of the Boston *Globe*.

16

Gerard O'Neill Becomes Less Convivial as Each Story Progresses

Boston *Globe* Spotlight News Team members can tell when things are normal for their editor and investigative colleague, Gerard O'Neill.

He becomes "less convivial as each project progresses," he admits. But they understand. They've been there before, too.

Gerard's projects—whether they are urban housing or phony vocational schools—blot out his days and consume his energy. Sometimes they leave him so exhausted he begins to question himself and the original thesis. Each experience, furthermore, can take its toll on interpersonal relations.

"We follow a fairly consistent pattern after deciding that there is a story," he says, outlining the work of the team. "Usually it's based on a tip. We begin by building a composite profile of the subject, keying on business interests, relatives, and personal life. Among the invariable public record sources we use are the Registry of Deeds to check land holdings, corporate records to determine business relationships, and vital statistics to chase down family trees. Then we cross-file everything."

At that point, he continues, the team is ready to talk with people. "We start with known enemies of the subject and, if he's in politics, there's never a paucity of enemies. These interviews are used to expand and verify information we've already gathered. Then we interview friends of the subject who, many times, are at least tangentially involved. One approach usually is to help us or else. It's not something we enjoy using but sometimes it's necessary. It also serves to disconcert the main subject who will hear from his friends and have loads of time to fret about his turn. Then we have the main confrontation interview."

The interview can be explosive—most frequently a tense atmosphere—because of the team's strategy. "We go armed to the teeth. We usually have 95 percent of the information needed and the interview is to try to catch the subject lying; explain things we are not totally sure of and to obtain quotes for the story in the hope it will have the subject trying to explain away the unexplainable—things we can contradict with other sources or documents. If he lies, we let it be and contradict the subject in the story."

The *Globe* reporters go to the interview convinced they have the upper hand. "It follows months of groundwork. But our approach is totally low key. 'We have evidence that may indicate wrongdoing on your part, but we want to give you this opportunity to correct any misunderstanding we may have' is our kind of approach. We go in with confidence that we know what we want to do, yet we try to avoid looking arrogant. We always at least try to avoid looking arrogant. We always at least try to use a tape recorder and we always have two reporters present at the interviews. Sometimes we take documents and pictures to press a point and unnerve the subject if we have to."

Does the strategy work?

The results show it does. In 1972, the Spotlight Team—O'Neill, Timothy Leland, Stephen A. Kurkjian, and Ann DeSantis—won the Pulitzer special local reporting award and Sigma Delta Chi's distinguished public service prize for its exposure of corruption in Somerville, a community of 95,000 on Boston's north side. It was an impressive feat for the Boston reporters if you consider the competition. It was the year Richard Cooper and John Machacek won local reporting recognition for their superb stories in the Rochester *Times-Union* about the Attica prison riot and it was also the year the New York *Times* and reporter Neil Sheehan were honored for their efforts in publishing the Pentagon Papers.

Said the Sigma Delta Chi judges, however, of the merits of the *Globe* investigation: "It brought the eventual indictment of three former mayors, the local auditor, and public works chief. Perhaps more important, it prompted strong citizen support of the current mayor's efforts to reform the city's government."

The Spotlight team became interested in Somerville problems when a citizen's group charged that community officials were allowing patronage and favoritism to influence the awarding of contracts. Spotlight members spent three months investigating the group's charges and digging further into Somerville affairs. They found more than they bargained on as a result. They uncovered a decade of corruption that, said Sigma Delta Chi judges later, "helped push this town to the brink of financial collapse despite one of the highest property rates in the state."

It was the kind of time-consuming, mind-boggling examination that can exhilarate and exhaust at the same time. *Globe* investigators culled six thousand public records and interviewed one hundred twenty persons before the first of six stories appeared in February 1971, disclosing what the citizen's group had feared: political favoritism toward certain contractors, conflicts of interest in tax assessments by some office holders and questionable practices in dispersing municipal finances. The Spotlight stories brought action. Within months, a grand jury had handed down one hundred nineteen counts of conspiracy against nineteen people and four companies. At the same time, the Massachusetts Legislature, shocked by the disclosures, drafted legislation aimed at controlling expenditures in localities throughout the state.

The "Spotlight-on-Somerville" series was the first of four investigations the team worked on in 1971 and all produced either legislative measures or follow-up inquiries by law enforcement offices. Tim Leland's Spotlight concept, introduced in September 1970, after he returned from a sabbatical in England observing the London *Times*' successful "insight" operation, had surpassed expectations in the *Globe* newsroom.

It wasn't the first Pulitzer for Editor Tom Winship's Boston staff, though. In 1966, a year after he was named editor, the century-old daily won the Pulitzer Distinguished Service Award for its coverage of the controversy over President Lyndon Johnson's efforts to name Municipal Court Judge Francis X. Morrissey to the post of U.S. district judge for Massachusetts. *Time* magazine credited Winship with providing the impetus to the *Globe*'s success and named the paper the most improved in the country. In 1974, the magazine listed the *Globe* among its newspaper top ten.

But that doesn't surprise newspaper watchers either. The *Globe* has been a successful publication since its first days in 1872. When General Charles Taylor became its publisher five years later, he made it more appealing and even more lively. Besides cutting its prices and establishing an evening edition, Taylor was responsible for enlarging the paper's headlines and local news coverage. Its content and mechanical department improvements were impressive. Publisher William Randolph Hearst visited Boston and studied the paper during the 1890s to find ways to use its innovations in his circulation battles with Joseph Pulitzer's New York *World*. The *Globe* ranked among the top ten nationally before the turn of the century.

Such traditions are daily reminders to O'Neill as he scrutinizes story ideas. And the scrutiny frequently comes down hard on some of Boston's businesses and institutions. For example, the *Globe* team's probe of vocational schools in 1974. O'Neill and Spotlight staffers spent the winter months examining trade, professional, and technical schools, their offerings and student recruitment. The key to assessing the quality of education among schools that offered such a diversity of courses as bookkeeping and truckdriving, they discovered, was the percentage of students who completed their studies and the percentage who found appropriate work. The series brought lawsuits, accusations, and countercharges. It also brought about new state and federal legislation.

Preparing such explosive articles takes planning. The *Globe* unit, he explains, organizes a story file which is prepared near the end of the preliminary period of each project. "Actually the file contains memos put together for easy reference. These items are ones we are sure will have a place in the story. Before we write, we read all of the story file memos to come up with an overview. The piece usually springs from an outline of main points discussed before the writing begins."

The Spotlight editor knows the size and shape of the finished article before the first word is set in type. "The pieces are usually a full newspaper page with pictures and are written with an overview lead naturally keying on one or two main points that underscore the whole project. Because of their length, the stories call for great care in making them readable. Strong emphasis on transition paragraphs when moving from one 'finding' to another and a certain amount of repetition on key points help the reader digest invariably complicated content."

The first draft is usually completed in about two weeks. Each member of the team reads the piece to double check on accuracy and to exchange ideas on style and structure. "Then the stories are read by the *Globe*'s libel lawyers and a copy editor is assigned to the team fulltime until the story is set," Gerard points out. "Actually, 70 percent of the work is in research and only 30 percent is spent on writing and polishing."

Gerard doesn't think in terms of a particular type of reader who might be interested in such a story; it's just not possible, he says. He's more concerned about the quality of content. "We just try to make technical, complicated data into a readable piece with emphasis on clarity and supporting sidebars." His tools are awareness and perception.

At a Boston School of Communication seminar not long ago Gerard told students women could have a real edge in getting sources (although there are few women at present among investigative reporting teams), and sources remain one of the most vital ingredients in the business. "Women sometimes appear less threatening," he explained. "A hard-nosed approach is less effective with some people. The benign approach can sometimes be better. A woman can use her wiles and what's the matter with that? You should use every attribute you have."

The investigation of fraudulent vocational schools was Gerard's most rewarding story. "I think it did the most good. It brought the biggest response certainly ... which can be the investigative reporter's best measurement, I suppose. I believe an investigative team—or a reporter for that matter—must be left alone to do the work. Judge their final draft as the sole product of their efforts. This is, happily, the case at the *Globe*."

While he enjoys his work and he believes investigative journalism "will prosper" during the next decade, he's surprised by those who equate journalistic achievement with large salaries or financial success. "It may happen to a few, I suppose, but no one can really expect much financial success—as it's known today—in newspaper work."

The comment comes from experience. Gerard started in journalism as a copyboy at the *Globe* and worked his way through the suburban desk, city hall, and statehouse beats to his present position. A Bostonian by birth, he went to Stoughton High School and later graduated *cum laude* from Stonehill College in Easton. He returned to the city and graduated from Boston University with a master's degree in journalism. Gerard won a *Globe* summer internship in 1966 and then served briefly on the news staff of the *Patriot Ledger* in Quincy. Shortly after he joined the *Globe* he received the United Press International Civic Service award for articles on a Boston school committeeman and city contractor.

He and his wife Janet and their son Brian live in North Easton, a community of four thousand, a good commuting distance from the city.

His satisfaction? "Changing things, really; making news instead of reacting to it. I'm doing what I always wanted to do."

Spending a day with the *Globe* editor gives one a sharply different view of the life of the investigative reporter, however. There's routine—"like firemen, we're not always putting out major blazes," a reporter quips—tension in the office among coworkers at times, and continual telephone conversations; endless talk which would probably bore the average person. Taking a recent day from his log, Gerard recounts:

"I started as I frequently do by driving my son to nursery school. When I got to the office I mediated two conflicts on the investigative staff. I got tentative consensus on methods to investigate a new project; justice at the district attorney's level. I called up two good potential sources and talked with them for a while. Then I went home early."

Gerard shares his successes, frustrations and disappointments with his wife. "It helps relieve the kinds of tensions that could come about without some kind of release, I suppose. I bellyache at home. At work? I fight."

Photo of Stan Penn courtesy of the *Wall Street Journal*.

17

Documents Are Crucial to Stan Penn's Stories

What amazes *Wall Street Journal* investigative reporter Stanley Penn is that it seems he'll never run out of stories about illegal activities in high places.

"I've been in the business a long time—twenty-three years—and I continue to find it incredible how widespread is corruption in business and politics. For me, the pleasure comes from digging out the story and exposing the wrongdoer."

He has made his mark, too. Among professionals he's considered a "thorough, methodical reporter—scholarly in approach—who spends more time in New York City's Federal Building than some of the people who work there." Nick Gage of the New York *Times* believes Stan is a professional's professional. "Stanley will go through files in every case. Just in case something has been misfiled or there's a bit of information in the deposition overlooked ... stuff like that. He really works at it. He's like a cop who works fraud cases and he's always going to sharks and checking fences and going to pawn shops . . . just nosing around."

Stan Penn, born and raised in Fun City, educated at Brooklyn College and later, the University of Missouri's prestigious School of Journalism, has had the successes many in the field only read about. His explanation? Attitude and more work than most people are willing to give to one project or task.

"I'm happy doing what I'm doing. I get a good salary. I'm left alone. To me, this kind of work is a lot more satisfying than handing out assignments or overseeing a news operation," he says. "For a while, some years ago, I had a beat and I was in charge of a few reporters, often including a brand-new reporter with little or no experience. I chafed at having to read the inexperienced reporter's copy or having to fix sentences. I felt, rightly or wrongly, that I was wasting valuable time that could have been used for turning out my own stories. I make demands on myself to dig and produce the very best and most authoritative pieces I can. To process the work of others just didn't satisfy me."

Stan's investigative materials fill volumes and filing cabinets. They include stories about city fraud, state and federal corruption, and international fraud, corruption, and theft. In most, his efforts have brought action . . . sometimes results.

"The stories that give me the most satisfaction were the corruption stories that a colleague and I did on the Bahamas in 1966. The pieces led to a Pulitzer in 1967 for national reporting for me and former colleague, Monroe Karmin, now an editorial writer for *Newsday*. They gave me pleasure for two reasons: we exposed wrongdoing on a grand scale and, second, the stories had impact. They helped kick out of office a corrupt government in an election held in January 1967, several months after our stories were published and had kicked up a big controversy in the Bahamas."

The articles told how the white merchant-politician minority of the United Bahamian Party, known as the Bay Street Boys, ran the islands, at the time a self-governing British colony with an 85 percent black population. The Penn-Karmin stories probed and publicly examined evidence that an American businessman and resort operator had paid fat "consulting" fees of nearly $2 million to members of the government's all-white cabinet in return for gambling permits. The *Journal* investigation revealed what a Royal Inquiry Commission from London later indicated; collusion among businessmen and government heads had enticed big-time gambling, including underworld types under indictment in the United States, to flourish and even settle in the islands, a place that attracted between 600,000 and 700,000 tourists— mostly American—annually.

"The Bay Street Boys, led by Sir Stafford Sands, then minister of finance and tourism and the most powerful figure in the islands, and Sir Roland Symonette, then premier, were ousted in the January 1967 election of Prime Minister Lynden Pindling, the first black head of the Bahamas. The Progressive Liberal Party got an 18-to-18 tie with the United Bahamian Party in the House of Assembly. The Bahamian Labour Party's only assemblyman, Randol Fawkes, cast the deciding vote when he broke the deadlock in favor of the PLP. The one-vote majority, however, was a clear victory for island blacks. The all-white cabinet was replaced with an all-black one which was sworn to a new code of ethics including financial disclosure and avoidance of conflicts of interest. The islands became independent in 1973. Karmin and I discovered that the stories we did were circulated in the Bahamas, mostly by the black taxi drivers, and excerpts were read by clergymen in the heavily attended black churches in Nassau, the Bahamian capital, and other towns," he says in reconstructing the investigation.

But Stan's efforts have also been counterproductive on occasions. A successful investigation and presentation of the facts have sometimes resulted in apathy or worse, criticism and rejection of his conclusions. Although frustrating and demoralizing, he accepts such response or lack of it as final decisions, beyond his control or influence.

When former President Richard Nixon nominated William Casey as head of the Securities and Exchange Commission, the *Journal* Washington Bureau received a tip: Casey may have been involved in questionable activities. It was Penn's story from the beginning. The reporter's sources showed that Casey was a wealthy man who was financially involved in a number of small electronics firms that sold stock to the public. But Penn's contacts had drawn a blank about the man otherwise.

Assuming that a rich man involved in many enterprises might have had a lawsuit or two over the years, Penn went to the federal court to check. He was right, too; there were several, including a plagiarism suit dating back to a time when the prospective Nixon appointee was a publisher. Stan also discovered that another suit involving Casey had been settled years earlier. Some reporters might have stopped there, assuming one more litigation would be a waste of time unless the material was readily available. Stan, however, knew that earlier suits were stored in a warehouse in Greenwich Village. He visited the warehouse and checked the file. It confirmed his suspicions. Reading over the transcript, he discovered that Casey had been accused by a stockholder of violating one of the securities laws he would have to enforce as chairman. The suit alleged that Casey had given the plaintiff information which led to a large investment in a Casey firm. The stockholder became dissatisfied and filed a litigation. The case was settled out of court.

At that point, Stan confronted Casey with what he had gleaned from court records and other sources. It was proper procedure for the *Journal* investigative reporter. He rarely goes to the subject he's writing about until he has all the hard information he can find to substantiate his case. "I rarely want to try to bluff anyone. He may just lie to you. It doesn't serve any purpose—so I go to see someone when I've got plenty. In my opinion, you go to the person last, though."

But hard information didn't bother Casey. He told Penn the litigation was a nuisance suit. Furthermore, he really wasn't close to the company involved, he said. Yet the reporter told *New York* magazine writer Robert Daley in 1973 he knew that Casey's law firm was general counsel to the company and, in addition to owning stock, the Nixon candidate was a director on the company's board.

A reporter's evidence and persuasion, however, doesn't always convince. "As a result of my piece, the Senate Banking Committee decided to take another look at him. The result was that they cleared him anyway and the Senate later confirmed him."

While disappointed, the forty-seven-year-old investigator is nevertheless a sober realist about his obligations. "I don't put words on paper until I have real documentation," he declares, adding that he is aware that the subjects of his investigations are usually personalities—rich generally—and their defense even in nuisance suits can be costly. Consequently, he insists, you've got to be cautious and fully comprehend the responsibility you have as a reporter when dealing with an individual's reputation.

Although he has never been sued, he has waged full-scale investigations that have raised serious questions about major figures and corporations in the pages of the *Journal*. "Many of the pieces I've done have involved offshore mutual funds and banks that collapsed, in large part because of the avarice of promoters and other businessmen who duped investors into putting their savings into these sleazy operations and who then looted the firms of their assets. Often, politicians eager to make a buck willingly join these outfits, thereby giving the firms some respectability. As a kind of example: I've done some pieces on how promoter Robert Vesco looted the IOS mutual funds of hundreds of millions of dollars (The SEC exposed Vesco when it brought an action against him in 1972). Vesco fled to Costa Rica, where he is now, and was befriended by then Costa Rican President José Figueres, considered a good friend of the United States and perhaps Latin America's best known liberal.

"I did a piece in 1973, based on documents I found in a federal court in New York City, that showed that Figueres had given Vesco a haven in Costa Rica. That money, according to the documents which Figueres didn't deny, came from Vesco-linked companies in the Bahamas and Costa Rica. Doing a story like that is what makes my job really pleasurable."

There are moments when it's more exasperating than pleasurable. Investigative reporters have to get used to verbal assaults and occasional threats, but the intensity in high places is sometimes surprising. After Stan's story involving Figueres was published, he called the Costa Rican president to check out still another story. The indignant head of state took the call, hissed "Go to hell," and hung up.

Attorneys can be difficult and threatening, too, when it serves their purpose. While combing the files in 1967, the Pulitzer winner found a suit by Allen & Company of New York against Occidental Petroleum. "Allen & Co., investment bankers, claimed that Occidental had screwed them out of their share of oil concessions in Libya. A French swindler was supposed to be involved. This intrigued me."

Confident that when the case went to court it would be a major litigation, Stan began acquiring data. During the next five years he regularly checked the courthouse to see if any pretrial depositions had been filed pertaining to the case. The court clerk became familiar with Penn. Stan, at the same time, ingratiated himself with the courthouse employee. He offered to search the records himself freeing the clerk to relax.

Then one day in late 1971, Stan scored; a sworn deposition from the former oil minister of Libya claimed he had been a close friend to an Occidental promoter in Europe while the bidding on concessions was in progress. Two of the best concessions, the former minister said, had gone to Occidental. Stan found the deposition by accident really. Such data, he knew, were usually sealed and kept in a judge's chambers. While the clerk read a magazine, the sharp-eyed reporter took down the information in longhand.

His story several days later raised speculation that the oil company had obtained concessions by subterfuge. Meanwhile, the political climate in Libya had changed and many were purged. A prominent attorney, representing Occidental, refused to give Penn any information and suggested that the reporter's story might harm the company. If there was any damage, the lawyer said, the *Wall Street Journal,* the stalwart of the business community, could be sued.

"It was a solid story. I found out from court depositions that the brother-in-law of the former oil minister had received a financial interest in a Liechtenstein construction firm controlled by a European promoter who had dealings with Occidental. At the oil minister's request the promoter had financed a $100,000 movie extolling

Libya for which the former oil minister wrote the script. The former minister claimed he took no money for the script, but his brother-in-law was to get 90 per cent of any profits the film might make, according to the deposition."

While a number of his colleagues prefer face-to-face interviewing, Stan has developed a strong attachment to the telephone. "Generally, most of my interviewing is done on the phone. It saves time. I'm a pretty good interviewer on the phone and often I can get good stuff that way. I save the person-to-person interviews for vital people whom I've never seen before. These people, because they've not dealt with me before, feel better if they can see me in person. They tend to trust me more, I've found, than if they just listen to a disembodied voice on the phone."

His work habits he describes as erratic. "I mean I really work in spurts," he explains. "When I'm on a story, I go at it full blast. I don't like it to drag on. Always in the back of my mind is that somebody may beat me to it. I've never lost that sense of the necessity of being competitive, I guess."

He tries to separate his work from his home life, but not by design. "I don't go into great detail with my wife on a story I'm working on. I'm not sure why, though. I suppose I'm in no mood to discuss it when I finally get home. When it runs, I'll often discuss with her how I did it, or the problems I had getting the information."

How does he see himself?

"I can't be classified as a loner or a private person. I'll usually mention a piece I'm doing to a few colleagues as well as the news editor, who is my immediate boss. I don't want to suggest fake humility when I say I don't see myself as any more important than a reporter who covers economic news for the *Wall Street Journal* or the guy in Detroit who writes about autos. In one way, perhaps, the investigative reporter is different from others.

"The night before a piece runs that exposes some wrongdoing, I get a little tense. I don't know if others have that kind of gut reaction to their stories. My reputation and the paper's are on the line, I believe. That's a sobering thought. I'm going to look like a fool if my piece that appears the following day isn't correct. We—the paper and I—could face a libel suit. Worse, if I'm wrong in any major particular, I'm going to have doubts about myself. So, until that piece runs and there aren't any kickbacks, I walk around with a queasy feeling. . . . "

More important, he contends, investigative reporting, regardless how good, must be kept in perspective by newspaper management. "Investigative pieces like the ones that the Washington *Post* did on Watergate are obviously something special. But, generally, I don't see the investigative piece as superior to a closely reasoned analysis of the economy or why we got stuck in Vietnam. The investigative reporter is a part of the group. If a newspaper carried only exposés, the public would have a warped view of what makes the world tick."

Success has wiped out insecurities for Stan Penn but it hasn't eliminated the dreams he once had. His realism has, however.

"In my teens, I saw myself as one day writing fiction. I found out later I had no real talent for it."

Photo of Jim Polk courtesy of NBC News.

18

Jim Polk Works Hard to Fit the Job to the Family

Some investigative reporters are convinced marriage and kids don't go with the job. They've tried and they've failed.

Others, however, have worked at both and found acceptable solutions. They've applied two reportorial ingredients—tolerance and perseverance—to make it work. An example: NBC investigative reporter Jim Polk, once a prize-winning newspaperman for the Washington *Star*.

"Work does not mesh with my wife and two kids. I've got a son, eleven, and a daughter, seven. I often work weekends. And I have to travel quite a bit. My wife, in fact, just started her own career as assistant school administrator," he explains.

"I try to make up for my absences by taking one member of the family at a time on a separate trip each year. Three examples: when working on a story on the coast in December 1971, I flew my son out to Los Angeles for the weekend and then took him up to San Francisco to see the Washington Redskins in the NFL playoff game. In 1973, I met a source at the Miami International Airport to get secret White House money records, and right beside me was my daughter (then five) and her stuffed panda. Last winter, I took my wife along on a speaking trip to Mexico City."

The affable newsman may be one of the few Washington investigative reporters who have doubled as a baseball manager. "I've found time for the last three years to manage my son's Little League baseball team. I flew all night back from Los Angeles for the playoff championship game one year. But in general, work does take precedence over family, and the two do not mix very well. This is not the fault of the profession. I think it can be ascribed to the nature of persons like myself who enter the profession, strive to be good in it, and thrive on it."

Journalistic awards demonstrate his success at "it." While he was national political writer for the Washington *Star* he won the 1974 Pulitzer Prize for his penetrating investigation of the 1972 presidential campaign financing. His stories, similar to those of his Washington counterparts Bernstein and Woodward, led to indictments against several Nixon cabinet members and campaign convictions. His painstaking research and writing have earned other honors. His stories have won the Sigma Delta Chi Distinguished Service Award for general reporting and the Raymond Clapper Memorial Award for Washington reporting, among others.

"But I don't like to rank stories," he insists. At the same time he admits there have been several that he remembers so vividly the minutiae come back to him as if they happened yesterday. "The disclosure of financier Robert L. Vesco's secret $200,000 cash contribution during an SEC fraud probe certainly stands out for me.

Then there was the first disclosure of presidential attorney Herbert Kalmbach's role as the secret Nixon fund raiser (which occurred several months before Watergate) ; a story I did on then Representative Gerald R. Ford's concealment of campaign funds in his 1970 House race; several articles on kickbacks in the state house administration of Alabama Governor George C. Wallace; a story way back in 1964 disclosing U.S. nerve gas production at Newport, Indiana, and stockpiling in rockets and other weapons. I believe I'm still the only reporter ever to get access for an inside inspection of a nerve gas factory. In general, whatever stories advance the public's knowledge about the private workings of government, those have been the most satisfying ones for me."

Colleagues believe Jim is a documents-oriented reporter who places less emphasis on source information. "Jim is an investigative reporter in the style of I. F. Stone. He reads, rereads, double and triple checks documents and his sources. My view of him is that he is the type of reporter who prefers to rely on documents and records, rather than strictly placing too much reliance on source stories or somebody's opinion of things. Example: So and So on March 15, attempted to pressure the Department of Defense to grant So-and-So a million dollar contract, according to reliable sources. No way, that's not his style. We have great admiration for Polk and for the *Star*, which gave him the time and space to do an excellent job," a Washington newsman says.

News professionals, both comrades and competitors, find Polk's attitude and definition of his field refreshing.

"Investigative reporting carries a sterner obligation that the reporter is responsible for the truth of every word in that article, that an allegation, a second-hand bit of knowledge is not immediately a fact. It is not always a starting point either. It is not a story in itself. You have to satisfy yourself that the content of what someone said is true. It is no excuse to come back later and say my sources were mistaken," Jim claims.

Grand jurors, for example, rarely provide solid information about a proceeding, even if you can get them to break their oath and discuss a case. "Grand jurors, I find, seldom listen that carefully. Actually you get more information and probably better quality material legally from witnesses," he adds.

Should a newsman be permitted to protect his sources?

Most couldn't function long unless they did protect their sources whether legally or illegally, he contends. "I am very leery of letting a legislature, particularly when it is often the subject of news stories, define the limits of the press and change them from year to year. That's what would happen, I think. I just don't want to open up the gates. I'm afraid that what is a blanket law one year would be amended the next."

Yet he admits that, at times, investigative reporting techniques protect the guilty as well as the innocent. "We're often involved in a sort of plea-bargaining—we don't name you, we keep your identity out of the embarrassment of what you've done if you tell us what you saw others do; what you were involved in first hand. It is not a particularly savory technique but one which we're involved in and one which bothers me, too."

Although his stories led to eight Watergate prosecutions, Jim's goal is not that of a crusader, a muckraker. "I don't believe the investigative reporter's objective should be to reform, or to prosecute, or even to get public reaction. His first, and only, purpose is to lay facts before the public so that it may be better informed—and let the public react to them in whatever manner it wishes, even including apathy, if it so chooses. The satisfaction is in lifting a corner of the curtain on various activities which a government or an official may at times conceal from the public it serves and to whose judgment it must be held responsible."

Nor does he believe a reporter should misrepresent himself. Some have. Reporters such as Harry Romanoff of the old Chicago *American* used voice disguises without leaving their newsroom desks. Said Timothy Ingram in a *Washington Monthly* article, April 1975, "Harry would work a phone twelve hours a day, masquerading as sheriff, governor, sympathetic stranger, or whatever character fit the occasion. After the 1966 mass murder of eight Chicago student nurses, he managed to get the gory details of the deaths from a policeman after introducing himself as the Cook County coroner, and to interview the mother of the suspect, Richard Speck, by pretending to be her son's attorney."

It's a question of ethics really, Polk suggests. "As reporters today we want open government and agencies and we demand the same of the people we interview. Then how can we support our own covert methods? I think its just as effective to tell people who I am and who I work for. When I start asking questions people generally start by explaining what they do and why. They don't want to be uncooperative most of the time. They think—and quite possibly they're right—they could make it that much worse by not answering the reporter's questions. The point is, instead of putting them on the defensive you ask them to help you better understand something—you'll get as much if not more than if you use deceptive means."

Jim has surfaced occasionally for the traditional press conference but most often sees such gatherings as a waste of time for newspersons, even presidential press conferences. "It only takes about two times to learn to field questions. If you don't want to answer them you talk about what you want to talk about.... There's not an easy way to shake a man without being argumentative. And that's frowned on. That puts the press in an antagonistic role with the president. The press is supposed to relay the news. The professional press doesn't boo or clap. In a televised news conference you don't talk to reporters, you talk to the viewers. He is trying to be open and accessible with guys who never go to Washington."

A typical day, Jim says, is frequently spent talking, exchanging bits and pieces with a variety of people, newspersons and broadcasters and those unidentified but ever-present people who are known to him as sources. "Take the first day of the week. It's a day when I start the whole process over usually. I schedule the coming days and do what is probably the toughest part of investigative reporting, looking for that spark which will turn into a story. The day—this particular day at least—included a talk with a federal investigator about a CIA tip. I checked it. It looked tenuous. It doesn't appear to have much to surface with. It's only peripheral to a current story. I probably won't pursue it.

"I called a federal prosecutor out of town to make an appointment to discuss with him an old postal investigation. On another story last week, I had run across a private reference that Gerald Ford might have been involved. Don't have high hopes for this one though. I found I have to spend three or four days making certain, checking it out. I had a long phone talk with one of my best Watergate sources. I conferred with my editors about a trip I want to take to the Northwest. I want to get a sealed court deposition that may involve a congressman. I also detected a pattern on one set of public records that I had only found twice before—but both of those led to prosecutions. I wanted to go knocking on doors to check it out. I can't promise anything, though. You never really know what you're going to find until you go out there and start to dig. Before I left the office I made a reservation at the Jockey Club for lunch the next day with an old contact."

But his working day still wasn't over. He circulated at a political cocktail party before he went home "to stay in touch with people—a very important part of this work"; and then he had a late dinner with his wife. He went back to work an hour or so later pulling out his records on a Securities and Exchange Commission tax case that he thought might come alive again soon.

"I don't think any good investigative reporter is a loner," he tells those interested in the field. "Not only does a reporter have to trust his sources (and be in a position to judge whether they are truthful), but the source must feel a trust for the reporter before opening up at all. Some have a lot to lose and their confidence rests on that trust. I'm quite independent, rather determinedly so. But I don't think I'm a loner. I've managed to keep personal relationships not only with sources, but often with the objects of my stories. I drink with other reporters, play poker weekly, have a rather active social life, enjoy the theater—my wife and I often take another couple as guests rather than going through the routine of giving dinner parties—ski and play tennis when I can take the time."

And what about the future?

"I have no desire to be an editor or a news executive. The professional satisfactions are in reporting, I think. The money and the prestige aren't missing either. As for power, that is an illusion in this profession. Any newsman who aspires to power in public as a result of his role is distorting his job to serve himself rather than the public. As long as I can still meet the demands—long hours and travel—and strains of the energy the work requires, I'd rather be...and will be...a reporter."

Photo of Jack White courtesy of Jack White.

19

Sources Can Make a Pulitzer, Jack White Says

Jack White's story in early October 1973, about President Richard M. Nixon's shockingly low tax payments of $792.81 and $870.03 in two successive years was like the tremor after the quake.

The Watergate investigation dominated the news when his investigative piece appeared in the Providence, Rhode Island, *Journal-Bulletin*. Within twenty-four hours, the story was clattering over the Associated Press A-wire about the president's 1970 and 1971 tax returns. The White House, bombarded with queries, refused to confirm or deny.

In November at a press conference, Richard Nixon admitted what White had written: he had paid only a nominal amount of taxes. A month later under mounting public pressure, the president made public his tax returns for the previous four years. Congress investigated. The Internal Revenue Service reexamined his case. And, while millions of Americans prepared their 1974 returns, Richard Nixon was informed by congressional and IRS investigators that he would have to pay $432,787.13 in back taxes.

The chronology of events doesn't impress journalists as much as the original story. An investigative reporter working more than four hundred miles from Washington had scooped the two thousand members of the Washington press corps. The result? A Pulitzer Prize in national reporting for an unknown Rhode Island reporter who had a source.

But how? most observers ask.

If you're a prober, Jack says, one or two reporters can get more tips than a whole pack of journalists. "Investigative reporting is just solid reporting with a different kind of approach." And he doesn't consider his Pulitzer Prize-winning story a real investigative effort. "The most rewarding story I've ever done was the Nixon income tax payment piece, certainly. But I don't consider that story a 'real' investigative project. The story involved some investigative techniques but it was really more a 'sources' story than a developed investigative task," the chief of the *Journal-Bulletin* investigative team replies.

"It was brought to my attention by some individuals. At the time this came about I was flying around the country between Providence and California, Washington, New York and Florida because I was off staff working on a story about navy cutbacks. In my travels someone I had known for a long time and who had been very useful to me said, 'You know, if you could see what Nixon pays in taxes you would be amazed.' And I was intrigued. I asked a few more questions. There were other people at the bar where I was talking with this person and they thought the same thing. Everyone was pretty insistent that I should make an effort. The person and others there obviously knew what I was going to find but couldn't help me in finding it. So I had to find my own way. Which, obviously, I did. And I got it."

Jack actually enjoys the kind of assignment that has day-to-day immediacy and which provides people with solid information they have an absolute right to know. A story he remembers as more satisfying than the Nixon piece was the announcement of military cutbacks in Rhode Island. The defense establishment was, for years, the state's largest employer.

"The military announced severe cutbacks at military installations throughout the country about two years ago," he explains. "I was called into a meeting with our top editors and discussed the situation. During the meeting it was decided that I would be 'off staff' for as long as it took to detail every facet of the military's pullout; the why, the cost, what it would mean to the economy and so forth. Everything."

For more than four months, the investigative reporter flew to virtually every corner of the country to talk with military officials and community leaders about the Defense Department's decision. And he wrote daily page one stories at the same time. "We managed to tell sailors who were leaving Rhode Island several things—including where they were going, when they were going, and what conditions at their new home port would be like. This was all done before the Navy told them."

Not everyone agrees, of course, that such stories form an investigative project. To Stephen Hartgen, author of "There's More Here Than Meets the Dragon's Eye" in the April 1975 issue of *Quill,* uncovering abuses or dealing with superficial questions is too frequently the reason for "investigative" reporting. Such assignments, he insists, emerge as problems quite close to the surface and relatively easy to expose. More important matters such as land-use patterns, criminal justice reforms, and more systematic kinds of issues are generally ignored.

But a story that aids people in making decisions about their future and well-being, Jack maintains, is worthwhile, too. He admits, however, his reasons aren't completely altruistic.

"For starters, I like the recognition. I can't deny that. And, it is really meaningful to get information people don't want you to have and perhaps correct some things that shouldn't be happening. Perhaps the most satisfying thing is that when you're done with a particular project, the project is done. You've been given the time and the money and you are able to say to people: 'This is the whole thing.' When you can give people the whole story in one package or a series, they really understand it. Of course, you don't always get the whole story either. It's nice, though, when you do."

Successful investigative projects aren't steps on a promotional ladder to higher editorial positions for Jack White though. "I don't want to become an editor in the traditional sense. Right now, I'm head of an investigative team. That gives me enough of the editor's role to play. So far, I have no complaints about the money. And as far as power and prestige, it depends on whose ballpark you're playing in. Those of us who do 'investigative reporting' have a tremendous amount of power. For good or ill, investigative reporters are around to do the 'heavy' stuff. What we write may result in the closing of banks, the ousting of politicians, etc. That, I think, is power."

Power to bring results, Jack insists, is what makes investigative reporting so satisfying. He has witnessed it in story after story. For example, Jack and a colleague were recently assigned to the robbery of a Providence bonded vault service when the story simply stopped for lack of information. "The Bonded Vault robbery stuff has been the hottest story around here in a long time," the investigator contends. "It started for us about a week after the robbery when several of our editors sensed it was a good piece that was going nowhere. They asked us if we thought we could do anything about it. Two days later, we obtained a confidential list of boxholders and we were off from there. We worked the story, dug out a lot of information and so impressed people who were involved that they ultimately became our sources."

The *Journal-Bulletin* investigative story, which first appeared nearly two months after the burglary, offered the public a closer look at the behind-the-scenes activity of a theft that was the second largest in the country's history (estimated take: over $3 million as compared with $2 million first announced). "We said very early that it was a multi-million dollar job, that the 'lead' man might want to make a deal and that there was a connection between the robbery and organized crime. When the man took the stand to turn state's evidence in the bail hearing for the other defendants he made us look pretty good. At least we think so," Jack recalls.

But stories about criminal activities and underworld figures bring certain risks and the reporter found out quickly how real the danger can be.

"When we went to Lowell, Massachusetts, to do a piece on the guy who surrendered, we received two very strange phone calls while in the detective division of the Lowell Police Department. It ended up with our getting a police escort back to Providence," he remembers. "Some guy who claimed to be Fred Smith from the Associated Press in Boston called the cops to ask if 'those two reporters from Providence are there.' No one but our immediate superior knew where we were. The detective said he didn't know but he would check. 'Fred Smith' hung up. He called again and when he was told he'd have to speak to the chief of detectives, he hung up. Boston AP has no one named Fred Smith. A guy named Fred Smith, a corporate executive in the Lowell area, had been killed months before by mob guys and he was cut into small pieces. The Lowell police gave us a two-car escort out of town. A Massachusetts state trooper picked us up outside of town and took us to the state line. A Rhode Island state trooper met us there and escorted us to the *Journal* building. Of course, if they want to get us they will. But everyone felt it best that night to at least get us back to Providence okay."

Prestige is the least of Jack's concerns. "I'd rather have a cab driver or a bartender tell me I did a helluva job than go to a cocktail party as an editor, let's say, and bask in the power of the paper's collective influence. Ultimately, I'd like to combine investigative reporting for the paper and work on a major book."

Each day begins with a familiar flurry for Jack and Beth White in their Newport home. It usually ends late. The catalytic developments occur after he finishes his grapefruit, says goodby to his family (three sons) and makes the daily fifty-minute drive from home to his office at the *Bulletin*. Most days can be exhausting, he says, recalling a recent twenty-four-hour period.

"I got to the office just after 10. Checked my mail first and secretary second for messages. There was some mail concerning recent stories on state investments and the favoritism involved. A couple of tips along these lines, but I didn't think they would work out. A note from the executive editor on a meeting to consider some changes in the afternoon paper. Meeting not until next week, thank God. I got a call from a local high school to be a commencement speaker in June. I accepted. I find I don't mind talking about what I do."

While waiting for Randy Richard, the other member of the *Journal-Bulletin* team, he thumbed through the file of story ideas reviewing in his mind the possibilities and priorities. They had just finished one major project and were about to polish the final draft of another. He felt comfortable when they had a couple of projects ready to go.

Just before noon, his partner arrives and the two reporters confer. "We reviewed our current project on how doctors play a role in hard drugs getting to the street. Randy brings me up to date on all the aspects he has worked on. We are ready to start, in a week or so, writing about our findings. And, as often is the case, we find our results interesting. The more involved we get, the the more interested we become in our findings."

The assistant city editor calls and wants to meet to talk about projects the paper's editors have talked about. The discussion continues for an hour or so and the first edition of the *Bulletin* arrives. Jack reads it over carefully looking for leads, tips, material other reporters have come up with while on routine beats or feature assignments that could aid an investigation in progress or initiate one. The afternoon mail brings more letters for the investigative reporters. "Guy from Warren, Ohio, wants an autograph. A couple of friendly letters and one from an attorney advising us that if we do what we plan to do on a particular story, we will violate the law. We had requested an opinion. He's not saying, 'No, don't do it.' Rather, he's just pointing out the pitfalls. We'll make a decision later probably."

Telephone conversations take up more than an hour as the afternoon slips by. And he still hasn't had lunch. But the phone calls continue. Jack sets up a meeting the next day "to meet a guy in a Dunkin' Donuts Shop." The source says he has some "good information." He won't know until he has talked with him. He makes a few more calls to check a number of possible projects. One involves trying to get a job with the Rhode Island Department of Natural Resources as a summer enforcement officer. "We have leads of information on how many positions are being created for politicians to dole out. We want to get the information firsthand. It means more phone calls."

Mid-afternoon and a note from another reporter tells the investigative team about an attorney who wants to talk about the shoddy collection practices of private bill collectors. Jack mulls over the possibilities in such a project and files it away for future reference. Randy, meanwhile, has gone out with another reporter to see what kinds of drugs the doctors will give them today.

It's near the supper hour in most homes and the investigative reporters are winding down a typical day. "There's some more paperwork and a few more phone calls yet. . . . We really need a research assistant . . . but they won't give us one. I haven't been out of the office all day. On the other hand, some days neither of us gets near the office. Leave about 7 P.M. and stop on my way home to get a sandwich which I eat while driving. Get to Newport just after 8 and pick up a six-pack of beer. I walk in the door just about the time Timothy, one year, goes to bed. Play with the kids, John and Pat, until they go to bed about 8:45. Tune in a Providence College basketball game on TV and relax a few minutes. Beth and I eat about 9:30. Beth goes to bed about 10:45 after we've discussed the paper she's working on in a graduate course in a local college. I review some of the papers—office work—I've brought home while watching the 11 o'clock news. About 12:30 I turn in, glad that payday is at hand and that those checks we've written won't bounce."

While he knows others who talk over their investigations with their wives, Jack doesn't like to bring work or its related problems home. The hour's ride to and from the *Bulletin* helps him sort out difficulties and adjust from one role to another. "I try to keep things separate," he elaborates. "However, there are nights when I get home that I have to talk to Beth about what Randy and

I are into or anything of special interest that we uncovered that particular day. Obviously, there are some things you don't talk about, but sometimes you feel that you have to spill your guts out." A bigger problem, Jack believes, is that he must go for days without seeing his three sons. "We try to make up for that at every possible opportunity," he adds, admitting that a day's work isn't that regular for an investigative reporter.

It's hardly the kind of work he expected to do in the late 1960s when he was a government and philosophy student at Boston University. He left BU in 1967 several credits short of a bachelor of arts degree. "I certainly didn't plan on being a reporter. I never worked on a school newspaper. But when I was in Boston I used to read four papers a day. I'd get the Boston *Globe* and the New York *Times* in the morning. I'd go to South Station which was the only place I could get the *Journal* the same day it came out. I liked reading the editorial pages," he says, musing about how he got into the business by applying for a job on the Newport *Daily News*. His mother, however, remembers an earlier time. He was twelve years old and it was Christmas. He received the tape recorder he had asked for so he could prepare the imaginary newscasts that kept him busy after school and on weekends.

"Jack White," says colleague Carol McCabe in a *Journal-Bulletin* story, "is usually smiling at the moment you look at him. He's the unintentional center of any group and he's the kind of man people confide in. Other reporters like as well as respect him; the two are not always synonymous in a profession built on competition and pressure."

Others sense similar qualities and are amazed. "Jack's unbelievable," says longtime friend Willie Blacklow who works in Washington. "He's a completely honest, fair, even kind of person. He's probably the only person I know who hasn't a single enemy in the world.

He is completely determined and when he wants to get something he'll get it, but he'll never sit around taking credit for it later." But Jack doesn't fool himself. "I'm outwardly open and smiling and everybody's nice guy. But inwardly, I'm very tense. Most of my pressures are self-generated, but they're there."

The work is demanding, the Pulitzer Prize winner continues, but that doesn't make him a loner. The more serious concern, he adds, is that small talk and too much exposure can lead to inadvertent slips about subjects you don't want to discuss. "And news really spreads quickly around a newsroom. You go to lunch with your fellow reporters but you really can't talk about what you're doing, in some cases. In other instances, it's obvious what you're doing and you don't have to 'avoid' conversations. Basically, when you're conducting an investigation you give the impression of being private, a loner type. That's because you're out of the main stream of the day-to-day, deadline-to-deadline, cycle of the paper."

If he wasn't an investigative reporter?

"I'd still be a private person. I don't like parties and get-togethers."

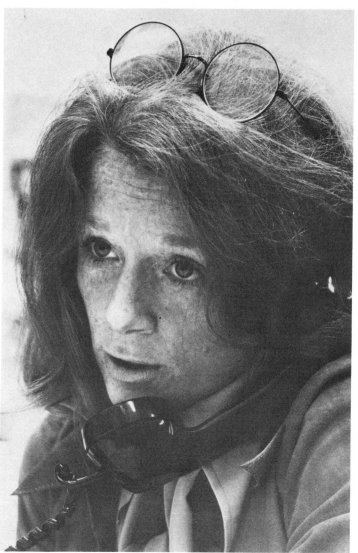
Photo of Pamela Zekman by Lynette Miller.

20

Pam Zekman Believes Satisfaction Is Better Than Any Awards

"Is the *Tribune* cool?"

The sales director of the Chicago-based correspondence school shrugged; he really didn't understand the salesman's question.

"Last year," the education peddler continued, "I was in the franchise business and the *Trib* had one exposé after another. It drove me out of business!"

And the Chicago *Tribune* didn't let him down again either. "We exposed his venture in the correspondence school industry, too," a satisfied Pam Zekman, former head of the *Tribune*'s six-year-old investigative task force, says. Her information, incidentally, came from an inside source. A *Tribune* reporter overheard the exchange between the sales director and the employe while applying for a job at the school to investigate the sales pitches used to recruit correspondence students. Such eyewitness accounts along with meticulous documentation go into every *Tribune* investigation before a word is set in print.

"We always worked on a project at a time for three to four months and then we published a week-long series of the findings. The series were characterized by under-cover work, an investigative tool that I think is one of the most effective," the thirty-two-year-old prize-winning reporter claims. She just recently joined the Chicago *Sun-Times* where she is continuing her investigative work.

The results support her contentions, too. Over the years, the series have resulted in legislative reforms, indictments, and other corrective actions which have brought frequent recognition in state Associated Press and United Press International public service and investigative reporting contests.

It was 1973, though, when the *Tribune* team received national prominence for diligent digging. The task force, directed at the time by veteran George Bliss, won the Pulitzer Prize in general local reporting for a series on vote fraud that resulted in more than eighty indictments of election judges and precinct captains. "The 1972 elections were the cleanest in anyone's memory," Pam recalls.

"In that project we worked as election judges to document fraud in the polling places on primary day. Through George Bliss, we then obtained a job in the Chicago Board of Election Commissioners' office for William Mullen (another *Trib* reporter)," she continues. In the months that followed, Mullen spotted hundreds of apparent forgeries on ballot applications. "The task force members then went out on the streets for months looking for people who had allegedly voted. The work was simply exhausting, the people difficult to find, but in the end we compiled what I think was an incredibly well-documented investigative effort," she says of the project. "It was rewarding because it was a topic that had been dealt with over and over again in Chicago, but never on this scale, and never with such lasting efforts."

Among the less celebrated but equally successful projects have been issues with state and national ramifications. For example, the *Tribune* task force's first assignment—nursing home abuses—exposed a controversy Congress and various state legislatures are still examining and trying to resolve.

"We worked in nearly twenty nursing homes throughout Cook County," Pam relates, "obtaining jobs as nurses' aides and janitors to document abuses that readers had complained about for years. The complaints had piled up because of the difficulty one reporter would encounter trying to investigate emotionally charged complaints of biased children and friends of nursing home patients. It was hard on us emotionally too. The only way to get an objective viewpoint, we felt, was to work in the homes ourselves. The filth and mistreatment that we witnessed were, at varying times, enraging and nauseating. It simply drained us. We each worked in about four homes for less than a week and we were able to document abuses in the care, feeding, and medications of senile and mentally ill patients to a degree. It wouldn't have been possible, though, without undercover work."

The series had a special exclusive each day: an eyewitness sidebar story accompanying the main article graphically depicting what the reporter had seen or experienced. In all, more than one hundred homes throughout Illinois were eventually closed in the wake of the investigation, including most of those *Tribune* reporters had probed. The closing of eighty homes beyond Cook County was directly attributable to the series, Pam insists. But there was a personal satisfaction for her, too. "One of the homes I worked in was considered one of the worst we investigated and I felt satisfaction unequaled by anything I had ever done when that place was closed down."

Sometimes investigations produced unusual methods in uncovering the bizarre or clandestine illegal activities. The team spent five months, for instance, documenting charges of brutality against members of the Chicago Police Department. The series brought action—along with hostility and praise—and it earned the *Trib* reporters the Edward Scott Beck award for their thorough investigation.

Like the vote fraud story, Pam remembers, police brutality was frequently discussed, but no Chicago media had really probed to find out more about the subject. "And like the nursing home story, it was extraordinarily difficult to investigate because the victims of police brutality were so emotionally involved that fact and fiction would get hopelessly entangled. We started with some five hundred names—and names only—of people who had filed complaints. We had to find them, investigate their charges by finding witnesses who were seldom anxious to cooperate. We wanted to use only the most clearcut cases of brutality, the cream of the crop we investigated."

The police department knew something was going on, but law enforcement officials didn't realize the extent of the problems within their ranks. Meanwhile, reporters found policemen aggressively defensive and verbally abusive when questions were asked.

Reporters worked in pairs in tough sections of the Windy City but they didn't know whether "people would quietly submit to questioning or shoot us." The reluctance of victims or witnesses to talk created a need for a different kind of reporting tactics and so *Tribune* staffers became witnesses, too. While one reporter talked with a subject another would remain just out of sight taking notes of the conversation. Reporters didn't use tape recorders because they didn't want to frighten away what witnesses they found. Instead, they wrote memos of what took place when they returned to the office. Meanwhile, the *Tribune,* determined to verify evidence, spent large sums of money to give lie detector tests to corroborate the information. In many of the one hundred ten complaints the reporters investigated, attorneys wouldn't let their clients talk to reporters because of pending lawsuits.

The team also discovered a number of complainants lived in fear or simply moved frequently. Seventeen homes or apartments listed as residences were vacated before *Trib* reporters arrived. The most brutally treated, reporters learned, were men, although women claimed they had been verbally attacked, and a few reported they had been shoved and threatened.

The first reactions to the six-part series were negative. Letters and calls in the first day or so were indignant that the police force was being berated. Then there was a change in the public response. Citizens began calling to offer more information about the cases mentioned in print and tips concerning others. The Chicago police, meanwhile, urged a new screening board be established and the Chicago Bar Association gave its support to a proposal to create an independent agency to investigate such complaints against policemen.

"The result was that we documented cases the police department had ignored. We also documented how the department had systematically phased out a psychological testing program once considered the best and most advanced in the country," Pam says. "The series resulted in three indictments (ranging from attempted murder to perjury), the resumption of a psychological screening program and transferral of police brutality investigations to a civilian review board."

Tribune reporters, on the other hand, have experienced the frustration of pursuing story angles that have led to a dead end. While working on the police brutality series, Pam continues, "We knew that each complaint we used in our series had to be perfect. If the police department found one hole in any single account they would drive a truck through the whole series. Half the reporting problem in a series like that is anticipating what the target of the investigation may come back with." But there were still near-misses.

"For example, one of the would-be brutality victims told us she had been held down on the ground by two large policemen after she unwittingly drove away from them when they tried to ticket her parked car. She was pregnant at the time, she said, and had a miscarriage two weeks later. We found several witnesses to the beating and they all confirmed that the policemen hit her unnecessarily and repeatedly kicked her while she was down on the pavement. It sounded like a terrific story. Particularly since she had a miscarriage," Pam explained.

"I decided to call the doctor to see if he would be willing to say the beating could have resulted in a miscarriage two weeks later. I doubted he would comment, as doctors are unwilling to comment about the weather usually, but it was worth a try. After much trouble, I reached him on the phone at midnight one night. He remembered the patient. I put my question to him: 'Would you say it was possible for her to have a miscarriage from the beating two weeks later?' My heart skipped as he seemed to agree: 'Yes, I would say it was possible.' Then he added, 'If she was pregnant. But she wasn't pregnant. She came in and took the test but never came back for the results. She wasn't pregnant.'

"Couldn't you just see our writing about a police beating that caused a miscarriage and the department coming back with the rebuttal that she wasn't pregnant?" Pam asked of no one in particular.

Another case involved a man who walked with a limp, talked with a slur, and acted strangely. He told the *Tribune* reporter who interviewed him that his condition was a result of shrapnel he took in the head while in the army during the Korean War. He had to fight his way back from total paralysis following the war injury, he claimed. Chicago policemen misinterpreted his slurred speech and limp. They thought he was drunk and mistreated him, the man said, while arresting him for disorderly conduct. "We verified his account of the story with other witnesses to the incident," Pam says picking up the story. "As the policemen grabbed him and were about to throw him (literally) into the squadrol he said he yelled at them: 'I fought for you and almost died for you and you shouldn't treat me like this.'

"Great line eh? We could just see it as a head to a vignette on this case," the *Tribune* reporter continues, taking a decided pause before she finishes her story.

"We had the case all wrapped up. We were ready to go with it when I thought we should verify his injuries with the army. I called the VA. They searched their files and found records on a Chicago man with the same name, but that man hadn't been injured. We went back to our victim and asked for his army number, etc. 'I don't give those out,' he said. We explained that we had to have the numbers or we wouldn't be able to use the story. Much to our dismay, he then sheepishly admitted that he never had been in the army. He had lied all of his life about the cause of his disabilities because he was embarrassed about their origin. He had gotten drunk with his buddies on senior prom night many, many years ago and was involved in a horrible car accident. Everyone else in the car was killed. He was paralyzed for years. Needless to say, we didn't use the story."

Other investigations have led to real life drama—life and death issues that created a sense of urgency.

On one assignment, Pam teamed up with former

task force chief Bliss to uncover a man posing as a doctor who had prescribed bizarre treatments and medications for mentally ill patients in a state institution. "Scores of deaths allegedly due to the medications had been called to the attention of state hospital officials, but they failed to act because they feared they could not prove the case and win a challenge the man might bring before the civil service commission," she points out. "The investigation was difficult because the impostor claimed to have graduated from the University of Havana Medical School, which we could not communicate with. But we tracked down former graduates of the school who helped us document that the university was actually closed down the year the man claimed to have graduated because of Fidel Castro's revolution."

The phony doctor was later indicted on charges of reckless conduct in several patients' deaths and treatments. He was convicted on one case and sentenced to prison with other charges still pending. The *Tribune*'s disclosures did bring about reforms, Pam says. "It's more difficult now for unlicensed foreign medical school graduates to work in public institutions in this area."

The awards, excitement, and prominence are reasons some investigative reporters give for pursuing explosive stories; but for reporters like Pam, there is a strong desire to help people who simply need help. "It may sound trite, but the kind of investigative reporting we did on the *Tribune* put us in a position of helping people who really had nowhere else to turn. They found themselves butting their heads against a brick wall, unable to get any satisfaction from their complaints. Or, they were people, such as nursing home or mental patients, whose voices were seldom heard outside the walls of the institutions," she continues. "On the other side of the coin, we also exposed both public officials and private businessmen who, for years, avoided public scrutiny. The exposure has been devastating in many cases."

The *Tribune* launched full-scale investigations against the small operator and the established community leader. "We did a full page layout about five franchise con men with their pictures and details of their sales pitches and how they were deceptive," boasts the diminutive reporter, one of the few women to serve as a task force chief on one of the country's major newspapers. "Exposure like that alerts countless consumers about them and other of their sort. In another case, we ran a series exposing the city's top ten slumlords and how they operate—men who for years had operated without anyone, including their tenants, knowing who they were or how much profit they were making off the misery of others."

What's a typical day like for Pam?

While it hasn't changed much in her move from the *Tribune* to the *Sun-Times* (both are morning papers in Chicago), there are no "typical" days actually, she says. Her workstyle, however, is different from the one she followed when she was task force chief. "When I directed the team, I had to divide my responsibilities between actual on-the-street reporting myself and orchestrating the activities of three other people. One day, for example, we had just finished a five-part series on trade and correspondence school abuses which had a considerable reaction. We were also already on the road to another project involving considerable undercover work. One member of my staff had been working undercover for a month— while the correspondence school story was being written —and had collected enough data to convince the editors that the project should be pursued. We don't talk about it elsewhere though; investigative reporters are quite paranoid about revealing the topic of a current investigation."

Pam's day begins about 7:30. An hour and a half later she's at her desk going over the morning papers. "I began this day by working out my story and background for a job interview I had that afternoon for our next project. I was applying again at an institution that had hired me five months earlier. I had not shown up for the job because we had to abandon the project temporarily," she explains. Poor economic conditions at the time had prevented other members of the team from finding work to pursue the investigation. "Now that some of the jobs started coming through, we decided it was time to try this particular institution again. I had left a telephone message at the institution explaining cryptically that I had been called home and couldn't start work right away. Now I had to return for another interview with the same woman and convince her that I wasn't irresponsible."

Pam spent the rest of the morning establishing her cover, reworking her background and résumé, and checking with people willing to serve as references. "There is a great deal of detail work to filling out these phony applications," she claims. "Even if they never check, which they rarely do, you have to be prepared for them to try and verify your background."

That chore completed, she began a review of the memo file of another staff reporter to complete a list of names the task force wanted to check with a state agency to determine if the people in question were properly licensed.

She went to the interview somewhat apprehensive. If the woman interviewer became suspicious how could she explain a five-month delay? Would the personnel counselor look over her background more carefully? Could she have used a few more references to support her case? "Incredibly enough, I got the job. I was to start in five days. Afterward, I drove back into the city to the state building and dropped off my request for information on a number of people we were investigating. The request involved considerable record pulling which the agency will do and then they let us know when we can come and review the files," she continued.

Returning to the office in midafternoon, she was told that the correspondence school series had brought results; one of the schools investigated—a major extension university—had fired much of its sales staff and several sales managers. The institution had refused during the *Tribune* investigation to be interviewed.

"Instead, perhaps appropriate for a correspondence school, they insisted that we submit questions in writing and they would answer in writing," Pam complained. "The procedure is just not as good as face-to-face interviews—they are much more effective, I believe—but we were forced to do it because they would have it no other way. We did our final interview that way and, of course, their responses ducked crucial issues. Now, with this new rumor, we called the school and again, they said they would respond in writing. Incredible! One hour later we got a hand-delivered letter refusing to comment on our inquiry and stating that personnel matters were confidential information. We then tried to verify our story through other avenues."

Late in the afternoon, the task force usually met to discuss strategy. "We communicated frequently when we were available. In this case, it was important. The following week, three of the four reporters on the task force were working undercover."

Meanwhile, task force members working in the office took calls and complaints on the correspondence school series then appearing daily in the *Tribune*. People called to tell their own "horror" stories or merely to seek advice. School owners called to threaten or accuse the reporters of biased reporting. Legislators from other states called to get copies of the series for guidance in legislation they were preparing to introduce in their own states. "We recorded the complaints, sent out copies of the series to those who needed it, refused to give advice or guidance on school matters, and stayed cool," she recalls.

Near the end of her workday, she made arrangements with the city editor to draw some money for an undercover assignment. Pam and the reporter went over the plan in detail with the city editor because of the preparation needed.

At 6:00 P.M., she left investigative reporting and the unfinished work on her newsroom desk and went to her art class for three hours. "It's one of my hobbies. Every Tuesday night I take a class and also try to paint at home when I have time. It's a great relaxer." After class she grabs a quick dinner and goes to bed. "Most days are such that I usually fall asleep after reading two pages of any book I take to bed."

While her family life has been altered by her work, Pam doesn't try to separate the two. "It's virtually impossible for me not to take my work home with me. We discuss it as a family," she says, adding that the difficulty daily is forgetting such absorbing work after hours. "If you're really interested you have to be willing to work nights, weekends, odd hours, sometimes without notice. That can throw family plans up in the air. You have to sacrifice a great deal of your personal life."

Does she see herself as an extroverted type who needs people around her continually or is she a loner who enjoys privacy and a very select group of friends? "I've heard that said about me—that I'm a loner. I don't think it's true but the description doesn't bother me if it's true."

Nor does she feel that there are obstacles she must overcome because she is one of the few women investigative reporters in Chicago, or in the country for that matter. "I don't feel any great difference being a woman in this type of work. I don't see where it is an asset or a liability compared with the men that I work with, with the exception that people are still less suspicious of women than men. This helps in getting jobs undercover and sometimes helps when the targets of an investigation underestimate you. I assume that more and more women will get into it simply because more women are becoming reporters. I have no advice for women wanting to get into the field that differs from that I would give men. It is very difficult to start right in as an investigative reporter. You have to be willing to start in any assignment and prove your skill at investigative reporting afterwards. Usually that means work on your own time as management is reluctant to give a reporter time for investigative work when he or she hasn't done it before."

And what about shield laws to protect reporters and their sources?

"I have yet to have a problem with a source who will not talk to me because of inadequate shield laws," she retorts. "I don't see that as a big problem. We have had to pause to consider the possible ramifications if we go forward on an investigation which might cause law enforcement agencies to want our notes and sources' names—but we have never had a serious problem with it." Management, she adds, has to stand behind the investigative reporter regardless of how much pressure a series brings. "That's of the utmost importance in this work. If I felt I was always on the firing line within the office as well as on the outside—if I was never sure whether I would be supported—it would be impossible to function, I think."

To Pam Zekman, the challenge of investigative reporting is to start with nothing or just tiny specks of information and build on it, working it, developing it from every conceivable point of view until she has constructed an "airtight" story. Yet it certainly wasn't a career goal she pursued while attending the University of California at Berkeley in the early 1960s. When she graduated with a major in English (she wanted a literature background), she really wasn't interested in writing. Returning home to Chicago, she spent a year as a social worker for the Cook County Department of Public Aid in the court services division handling child support, custody, and adoption matters. But it wasn't satisfying; it actually resembled clerical duties instead of case work. Without a degree in social work and no intention or desire to get graduate certification in the field, she suddenly realized there was no light at the end of the tunnel.

Casual conversation one day led her to the Chicago City News Bureau, a training ground for a number of young reporters—ambitious professionals such as Sy Hersh, for example. The News Bureau is like a local Associated Press or United Press International. It sends reporters out on assignments or gives them beats. Their stories are sent to local newspapers, radio, and television as well as wire services to use as a backstop. If the medium didn't cover the story, the City News Bureau did. Before joining the *Tribune* in May 1970, Pam got her chance to decide for herself if reporting was what she wanted. She covered criminal courts, police beats, and the State of Illinois building, and she spent two years on the federal court beat. Her last assignment was her most exciting: she covered the Conspiracy Seven Trial for the News Bureau.

"I never wanted to be an investigative reporter really until I fell into it. Now, I wouldn't want to do any other kind of reporting," she says with the excitement of a kid on Christmas day. You know she means it.

Notes

1. Jack Anderson

Anderson, Jack, *The Anderson Papers*. New York: Ballentine Books, 1974.

Anderson, Jack. "How I Became a Muckraker," *Argosy* (May 1974) : 25,26,52.

"Anderson Column Is Found Inaccurate," *Editor & Publisher* (February 15,1975) : 15.

"Anderson Denies Articles Favored Cuban Dictator," *Editor & Publisher* (July 14,1973) : 14.

Interview with Jack Anderson, Colgate University, March 4, 1975.

"Jack Anderson Has Interest in New Bank," *Editor & Publisher* (August 17, 1974) : 41.

Mutter, Edward. "Jack Anderson: The Evangelist Columnist," *Quill* (May 1972): 4–5.

Playboy Interview with Jack Anderson, *Playboy* (November 1972) : 87–91.

Sheehan, Susan. "The Anderson Strategy: We Hit You—
Pow! Then You Issue a Denial, and—Bam—We Re-
ally Let You Have It," *New York Times Sunday
Magazine* (August 13, 1972): 10, 11, 76, 82.

2. Bill Anderson

"Charges Against Reporters Dropped on a Technicality,"
Editor & Publisher (March 8, 1975): 10.
"400 Stories on Police Corruption," *Quill* (1975): 15.
"*Indianapolis Star* Series Exposes Police Corruption,"
Editor & Publisher (April 13, 1974): 9, 24.
Interview with William Anderson, August 5, 1975.
"Investigative Reporters Are Indicted," *Editor & Pub-
lisher* (September 21, 1974): 10.
"Justice Dept. Enters Indy Police Corruption Case," *Ed-
itor & Publisher* (December 21, 1974): 12.
"U.S. to Study Bribe Charges Against Newsmen," *Editor
& Publisher* (October 5, 1974): 10.

3. Carl Bernstein

The Associated Press Managing Editors Red Book. New
York: The Associated Press, 1974. Pp. 78–82.
Bernstein, Carl. "Watergate: Tracking It Down," *Quill*
(June 1973): 45–48.
Bernstein, Carl. Commencement address and interview,
Utica College, May 18, 1975.
"1700 Attend 14th Liebling Convention," *Editor & Pub-
lisher* (May 17, 1975): 34.
Simons, Howard. "Watergate as a Catalyst," *Montana
Journalism Review,* no. 18 (1975): 12–15.

4. Peter Bridge

Associated Press dispatch, "Peter Bridge," October 25,
1972.
"Bridge Leaves Jail Vowing to Continue in Journalism,"
Editor & Publisher (October 28, 1972): 9.

"Bridge Raps on Recent Jailing," Utica College *Tangerine* (November 10, 1972) : 1.

"Courageous Stand Not Easy to Take," The Oneonta *Star* (October 13, 1972) : 3.

"Imprisoned UC Grad Wins Aid," Utica *Daily Press* (October 11, 1972).

Interview (unpublished), Peter Bridge with Cynthia Bird, December 10, 1973.

Interview with Peter Bridge, August 17, 1974.

"Jailed Reporter Returns to UC," Utica *Observer-Dispatch* (November 20, 1972).

Memo (undated), Peter Bridge project, Utica College, prepared by Charles Kershaw.

"The Not-Quite Free Press," *Newsweek* (October 16, 1972) : 60.

"Reporter Will Go to Jail," Utica *Daily Press* (October 4, 1972) : 9.

"Threatened Reporters," *Time* (October 16, 1972) : 44.

"Urges Law to Protect Newsmen," Utica *Daily Press* (October 5, 1972) : 11.

5. Larry Brinton

"A Hard-Working Investigative Reporter Spurs Many Reforms," *Gannetteer* (July 1975) : 12–13.

Interview with Larry Brinton, August 6, 1975.

6. K. Scott Christianson

Christianson, K. Scott. "Albany's Finest Wriggle Free," *The Nation* (December 3, 1973) : 587–589.

_____. "Heroin & Corruption in Albany" (series of 16 stories), *Knickerbocker News* (October, November, 1974).

_____. "The New Muckraking," *Quill* (July 1972) : 10–15.

_____. "Rocky Asks for Mall Security Report," *Knickerbocker News* (May 19, 1971) : 1.

————. "Stratton and War, Inc.," *The Washington Park Spirit* (November 12, 1974) : 9.

————. "Way Beyond Good and Evil," *The Washington Park Spirit* (August 7–20, 1974) : 9–12.

Correspondence with K. Scott Christianson, March 31, 1975.

Slocum, Peter. "Reporter's Quest Now State Probe of Albany Politics." The Troy (N.Y.) *Times Record* (September 18, 1973).

7. Gene Cunningham

Interview with Gene Cunningham, June 12, 1975.

"Reporter Goes on Welfare to Document Irregularities," *Editor & Publisher* (March 17, 1973) : 19.

8. Ted Driscoll

Driscoll, Theodore. "ABA Gives U.S. Senators Report on Phoenix Deal," Hartford *Courant* (March 5, 1975).

————."Aiding GOP Registry Can Pay Off," Hartford *Courant* (May 14, 1973).

————. "Businessmen Reaping Profits by Leasing Buildings to State," Hartford *Courant* (March 3, 1974).

————. "Favoritism, Politics Break Law in Filling Numerous State Jobs," Hartford *Courant* (July 1, 1973).

————. "Republican Party and Connecticut Illegal Voter Registration Series," Hartford *Courant* (May 1973).

————. "State Knew Phoenix Broke Code," Hartford *Courant* (April 2, 1975).

Interview with Ted Driscoll, August 13, 1975.

9. Nick Gage

Daley, Robert. "Super Reporter... The Missing American Hero Turns Out to Be... Clark Kent," *New York Magazine* (November 12, 1973) : 46.

"Dispute on Investigative Reporting Leads Press to

Study Its Role," New York *Times* (December 2, 1974) : 29.

Gage, Nicholas. "Nick Gage Deals with Mafia Soldier— For Story, That Is," New York *Times Talk* (July-August 1975) : 1–2.

Interview with Nicholas Gage, May 1975.

Panel on Investigative Reporting: How It's Done, Over-Seas Press Club, New York City, January 7, 1975.

10. Jim Haught

Haught, James A. "Gov. Moore's Tax Case, 'Turkey, Not a Fix,'" Charleston *Gazette* (May 10, 1973).

_____. "Moore Tab $170,000 with Tax, IRS Says," Charleston *Gazette* (July 18, 1973).

Ingram, Timothy. "Investigative Reporting: Is It Getting Too Sexy?" *The Washington Monthly* (April 1975) : 61.

Interviews with James A. Haught, September, 1975; January, 1976.

Taylor, William D., American Newspaper Publishers Association Convention, New York City, April 22, 1974.

11. Sy Hersh

Daley, Robert, "Super Reporter . . . The Missing American Hero Turns Out to Be . . . Clark Kent," *New York Magazine* (November 12, 1973) : 42–48.

Downie, Leonard, Jr. *The New Muckrakers.* Washington: New Republic, 1976. Pp. 50–92.

Eszterhas, Joe. "Seymour Hersh, Toughest Reporter in America," *Rolling Stone* (April 10, 1975). Permission granted to use excerpts of copyrighted article.

Ingram, Timothy. "Investigative Reporting: Is It Getting Too Sexy?" *The Washington Monthly* (April 1975) : 54.

Interview with Sy Hersh, with Nancy Setapen, Spring, 1973.

————. "Such Trying Times To Be Raking Muck." *Quill* (December 1974) : 22–23.

12. Phil Meyer

Interview with Philip Meyer, March 1975.

Meyer, Philip. *Precision Journalism: A Reporter's Introduction to Social Science Methods.* Bloomington: Indiana University Press, 1973.

Riordan, Patrick. "Top Investigative Newsmen Tell 'Tricks-of-the-Trade,' " *Editor & Publisher* (January 6, 1973).

13. Tom Miller

"Huntington's Tom Miller Wins National Awards," *Gannetteer* (July 1975) : 20.

Interview with Tom Miller, August 12, 1975.

14. Clark Mollenhoff

Boston University School of Public Communication Seminar, April 23–24, 1975.

Correspondence with Clark Mollenhoff, August 5, 1975.

"Does the First Amendment Need Saving?" *Nieman Reports* (June 1973) : 9–10.

Huston, Luther. "Mollenhoff Says an Absolute Shield Would Hurt the Press," *Editor & Publisher* (March 10, 1973) : 8.

Letter from former Hartford *Courant* Publisher-Editor Robert Eddy, June 5, 1975.

Memo, Commodity Markets Investigation; Associated Press Managing Editors Public Service Award, 1975.

Mollenhoff, Clark. "Tells How Nixon Became Trapped," *Seminar* (December 1974) : 5.

15. Jack Nelson

Daley, Robert. "Super Reporter ... The Missing American Hero Turns Out to Be ... Clark Kent," *New York Magazine* (November 12, 1973) : 42–44.

"Dispute on Investigative Reporting Leads Press to Study Its Role," New York *Times* (December 2, 1974) : 29.

Huston, Luther. "Los Angeles *Times* Washington Bureau," *Editor & Publisher* (January 27, 1973) : 5.

Ingram, Timothy. "Investigative Reporting: Is It Getting Too Sexy?" *The Washington Monthly* (April 1975) : 60.

Interview with Jack Nelson, July 1975.

Investigative Reporting Panel, Sigma Delta Chi, Phoenix, Arizona, November 1974.

"Notes on 'The Biggest Bankroll Theory,'" *MORE* (May 1975) : 20.

"Such Trying Times to Be Raking Muck," *Quill* (December 1974) : 22–23.

16. Gerard O'Neill

Behrens, John. *Reporting Work Text*. Columbus GRID, 1974. Pp. 13–29.

Interviews with Gerard O'Neill, June-July 1972; June 1975.

"Municipal Reform Brings SDX Prize to Boston *Globe*," *Editor & Publisher* (April 8, 1972) : 9.

"Pulitzer Prize Winners," New York *Times* (May 2, 1972) : 36.

Reporting Seminar, School of Public Communication, Boston University, April 23–24, 1975.

17. Stan Penn

Daley, Robert. "Super Reporter ... The Missing American Hero Turns Out to Be ... Clark Kent," *New York Magazine* (November 12, 1973) : 45.

Hynds, Ernest. *American Newspapers in the 1970s.* New York: Hastings House, 1975. Pp. 263–265.

Interview with Stanley Penn, February, 1975; December, 1976.

18. Jim Polk

Fisher, Kathi, Craig Black, Ellen Debenport, Lilla Ross. "President Ford's Press Conference," *Quill* (December 1974) : 18–19.

"Hot on the Trail of Political Cash," *Quill* (June 1974) : 26.

Ingram, Timothy. "Investigative Reporting: Is It Getting Too Sexy?" *The Washington Monthly* (April 1975) : 56.

Interview with Jim Polk, March 1975.

The Investigative Reporter (panel), Sigma Delta Chi, Phoenix, Arizona, November 1974.

"Investigative Writing Fund Has Aided Successful Probes," *Editor & Publisher* (November 17, 1973) : 15.

19. Jack White

Interviews with Jack White, March 3, 1975; February 9, 1976; November, 1976.

McCabe, Carol. "The House in Newport Filled with Delight," The Providence *Journal* (May 7, 1974) : A–30.

"Pulitzer Prizes," *Quill* (June 1974) : 32.

20. Pam Zekman

"How Voting Frauds Were Uncovered by Chicago *Tribune*," *Editor & Publisher* (May 26, 1973) : 55.

Interview with Pamela Zekman, June 1975 and February, 1976.

"Omaha Sun Wins SDX Public Service Prize," *Editor &
Publisher* (April 14, 1973) : 13.

"Police Brutality Exposed by Chicago *Tribune* Team,"
Editor & Publisher (January 5, 1974) : 14.

Williamson, Lenora. "8 Newsmen and 3 Papers Are
Awarded Pulitzers," *Editor & Publisher* (May 12,
1973) : 12.

Bibliography

General References

Anderson, David, and Peter Benjaminson. *Investigative Reporting*. Bloomington: Indiana University Press, 1976.

Anderson, Jack. *The Anderson Papers*. New York: Random House, 1973.

The Associated Press Managing Editors Red Book, 1972. New York: Associated Press. 1972.

The Associated Press Managing Editors Red Book, 1973. New York: Associated Press, 1973.

Bernstein, Carl, and Robert Woodward. *All the President's Men*. New York: Simon and Schuster, 1974.

————. *The Final Days*. New York: Simon and Schuster, 1976.

Behrens, John C. *Reporting Work Text*. Columbus: GRID, 1974.

Copple, Neale. *Depth Reporting*. Englewood Cliffs, N.J.: Prentice-Hall, 1964.

Crouse, Timothy. *The Boys on the Bus.* New York: Random House, 1972.

Downie, Leonard, Jr. *The New Muckrakers.* Washington: New Republic, 1976.

Emery, Edwin. *The Press and America* (3rd ed.) Englewood Cliffs, N.J.: Prentice-Hall, 1972.

Hersh, Seymour. *Cover-up.* New York: Random House, 1972.

Hulteng, John. *The Messenger's Motives.* Englewood Cliffs, N.J.: Prentice-Hall, 1976.

Hynds, Ernest C. *American Newspapers in the 1970s.* New York: Hastings House, 1975.

Kaplan, Justin. *Lincoln Steffens.* New York: Simon and Schuster, 1974.

Krieghbaum, Hillier. *Pressures on the Press.* New York: Thomas Y. Crowell, 1972.

MacDougall, A. Kent. *The Press.* Princeton, N.J.: Dow Jones, 1972.

Meyer, Philip. *Precision Journalism: A Reporter's Introduction to Social Science Methods.* Bloomington: Indiana University Press, 1973.

Miller, Arthur R. *The Assault on Privacy.* Ann Arbor, Michigan: University of Michigan Press, 1971.

Pearson, Drew, and Jack Anderson. *The Case Against Congress.* New York: Simon and Schuster, 1968.

Pilot, Oliver. *Drew Pearson.* New York: Harper's Magazine Press, 1973.

Report of the National Advisory Commission on Civil Disorders. New York: Bantam-*New York Times*, 1968.

Rivers, William. *The Mass Media* (2nd ed.). New York: Harper Row, 1975.

Sellers, Leonard. "Investigative Reporting: Methods and Barriers." Dissertation, Stanford University, 1974.

Wise, David. *The Politics of Lying.* New York: Random House, 1973.

Articles, Working Papers

Anderson, Jack. "How I Became a Muckraker." *Argosy* (May 1974) : 25, 26, 52.

Arnold, Martin. "Recent Events Raise Practical and Ethical Questions about Some Aspects of Investigative Reporting." New York *Times* (April 28, 1975) : 23.

Bergman, Lowell; William Niese, Louis Loeb. "Libel Law Workshop." Urban Policy Research Institute, San Diego, California, January 10, 1976.

Christianson, K. Scott. "The New Muckraking." *Quill* (July 1972) : 10–15.

Cuyler, Lewis C. "Ethics of Investigative Reporting Questioned." *Editor & Publisher* (September 13, 1975) : 10.

Daley, Robert. "Super Reporter . . . The Missing American Hero Turns Out to Be . . . Clark Kent." *New York Magazine* (November 12, 1973) : 42–48.

Elder, Shirley. "Who's the Best Investigative Reporter?" *Washingtonian* (August, 1975) : 70–79.

Eszterhas, Joe. "Seymour Hersh, Toughest Reporter in America." *Rolling Stone* (April 10, 1975) : 48–52.

"Exploring Ways and Means of Increasing the Quality and Quantity of Investigative Journalism." A working paper, Urban Policy Research Institute, Beverly Hills, California, April 17, 1975.

Freivogel, Bill. "Public Affairs Reporting Assessed at Press Meeting." *Editor & Publisher* (November 3, 1973) : 7.

Gage, Nicholas. "Nick Gage Deals with Mafia Soldier— For Story, That Is." New York *Times Talk* (July-August 1975) : 1–2.

Hartgen, Stephen. "There's More Here Than Meets a Dragon's Eye." *Quill* (April 1975) : 12–15.

Hill, I. William. "Editors, Reporters Come Under Fire

at APME." *Editor & Publisher* (October 25, 1975):
12.
Ingram, Timothy. "Investigative Reporting: Is It Get-
ting Too Sexy?" *The Washington Monthly* (April
1975): 53–62.
Interview with Jack Anderson. *Playboy* (November
1972): 87–91.
Levett, Michael; Dan Noyes, Mae Churchill. "Exploring
Ways and Means of Improving the Art of Investiga-
tive Journalism." Urban Policy Research Institute,
Beverly Hills, California, October 18, 1974.
Mutter, Edward. "Jack Anderson: The Evangelist Col-
umnist." *Quill* (May 1972): 4, 5.
"The New Concerns About the Press." *Fortune* (April
1975): 121–23, 126, 128, 130–31.
Sheehan, Susan. "The Anderson Strategy: We Hit You—
Pow! Then You Issue a Denial, and—Bam!—We
Really Let You Have It." New York *Times Sunday
Magazine* (August 13, 1972): 10, 11, 76, 82.
Simons, Howard. "Watergate as a Catalyst." *Montana
Journalism Review* no. 18 (1975): 12–15.
"Slander Suit Imperils Investigative Reporting." *Editor
& Publisher* (February 2, 1974): 14.
Wilt, George. "Investigative Efforts Receive Scant Pro-
motion." *Editor & Publisher* (June 7, 1975): 32.
"Writer Must Pay for Lying to News Sources." *Editor
& Publisher* (February 8, 1975): 21.

Index

249